THE GRAND EXPERIENCE

THE GRAND EXPERIENCE

A drama in five acts
Containing a description of Wilmington's
Grand Opera House & Masonic Temple, a
Victorian Building in the Second Empire Style and
A history of the many parts it has played in the
Delaware Community for more than a Century

by

TONI YOUNG

Published by The American Life Foundation for
THE GRAND OPERA HOUSE, INC.
1976

© Toni Young, 1976

ISBN   0-89257-012-1

The American Life Foundation & Study Institute, Watkins Glen, New York 14891 published and distributes this book for THE GRAND OPERA HOUSE, INCORPORATED

First Edition. Two thousand copies printed of which the first three hundred are casebound, numbered, and signed by the author.

This is copy number

PROGRAM

Restored interior of The Grand Opera House, 1976

All the World's a Stage

Eugene Ormandy

And all the men and women merely players

A building is not merely a pile of bricks and mortar. It is the embodiment of the spirit of the people and activities that prosper in it. The story of the Grand Opera House is the drama of one building and the rôle it has played in the Delaware community for more than a century. In March 1872 famed Victorian tragedian E. L. Davenport came to the footlights at the close of his performance to praise the Opera House which "exceeded his views in every respect of what he had heard of it." He gave the people of Delaware credit for talent, wealth, and refinement. More than one hundred years later Mæstro Eugene Ormandy told a capacity crowd gathered in May 1976 for the re-opening of the Grand Opera House that the acoustics of the hall were excellent. He praised the sound on stage enabling the musicians to hear each other as well as the "bright, clean sound" projected to the audience. "I will record here anytime," said the renowned conductor.

The plot of *The Grand Experience* is simple. After the Grand Opera House was built as part of the Masonic Temple in 1871, it became an object of civic pride as the glorious setting for jewels of nineteenth century oratory, acting, and music and as the elegant home of distinguished businesses. This building enriched the architectural, cultural, and commercial life in Delaware for nearly forty years until it suffered tragic decline, deterioration, and disuse in the twentieth century as a motion picture theatre. Recently, heroic rescue by a brave group of Delawarians restored the theatre to Victorian grandeur so it could resume its rôle as Delaware's Performing Arts Center.

Numerous actors played in *The Grand Experience:* the Masons who envisioned a temple with a public theatre; the architects, contractors, and artisans who constructed an elegant Victorian building; the performers and tenants who prospered in it; the preservationists, architects, and craftsmen who restored the theatre; and thousands of Delawarians who were enriched by its offerings—each formed an entity known as Delaware's Opera House. In turn, the Opera House had a major impact on these groups—something intangible and ennobling called *The Grand Experience.*

8

E. L. Davenport

Man's life is fleeting. He is but "a poor player/That struts and frets his hour upon the stage/And then is heard no more." But a building endures. Because Delawarians recognized its rich heritage, the Grand Opera House continues to symbolize the ennobling tradition of the performing arts.

9

'Ere the play begins, let's set the stage . . .

Bird's-eye view of Wilmington, 1865

Strong prejudices against theatre prevailed in Delaware and throughout the majority of early colonial America.[1] Church and Puritan leaders feared that too much pleasure seeking and glorification of man would lead to his ruination. In 1774 Reverend Francis Ashbury was purported to have preached to a gathering of Delawarians that "Satan was there diverting the people with a play."[2] Despite the church's opposition to secular theatre, drama and rhetoric were integral parts of church ritual; and limited theatrical performances did flourish. (Hostility to the theatre still prevalent in 1870 was made even more vocal by the opening of the new Opera House.) Theatre was also shunned for patriotic reasons. The early American theatre borrowed heavily from the British tradition by using English plays, actors, managers, costumes, and sets. As an extremely patriotic state, Delaware was distinctly anti-British.[3]

Anti-theatre sentiment in Delaware resulted in relatively little theatrical activity well into the 19th century. The first known professional season was not held until 1827 when a Mr. Cowell of Philadelphia brought his Dramatic Corp to a tavern called Cross Keys.[4] While theatrical productions increased throughout the country as earlier colonial prejudices waned, entertainment in Delaware before 1827 was predominantly limited to scientific demonstrations, lectures, and menageries.[5] Although a second theatrical troupe performed at the Bayard Hotel in 1833, the first building devoted primarily to theatre was not opened until 1834. The Wilmington Theatre, located on the southeast corner of 6th and Shipley Streets, was not welcomed by the entire community: "a large number of citizens shook their heads in dismay and said the whole town was destined to go to ruin if so many of their friends and neighbors patronized so wicked a thing as a theatre."[6] One year later no plays were produced here during the normal winter season because it had become the summer adjunct of Philadelphia playhouses. The Wilmington Theatre disappeared before 1845, and Delaware had no permanent theatre for many years, despite the large external growth of theatres in the rest of the country between the Revolutionary War and 1850.[7] New York's first theatre (the Park Theatre) was built in 1789; by 1855 New York had eight theatres. Philadelphia and Boston experienced similar expansions. At the same time, theatre spread with the settlers to the mid-West and Far West.

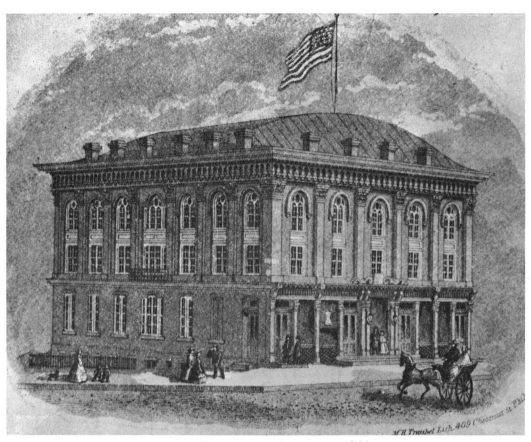

The Wilmington Institute, 1859

While theatre construction boomed throughout the United States, theatrical performances in Delaware were held in small buildings which could be adapted to dramatic purposes.[8] Occasional performances were given at the Academy of Natural Sciences, City Hall, or Temperance Hall. In 1847-1848, the Odd Fellows built a hall which included a small auditorium for public entertainment. In the 1850s, Union Hall, the Metropolitan theatre, and Chadwick Varieties and Museum at the Fountain Hotel also served as small variety theatres. The largest hall was part of the public library; although Wilmington Institute's hall could seat 1,000 people, it was criticized by some for a "look of bareness" and for very bad echoes "which rendered a speech unintelligible unless the hall was filled to capacity." [9] Despite the presence of these small halls, Wilmington had no building suitable for dramatic entertainment. Small wonder then that so many Wilmingtonians went to that place on the Schuylkill for entertainment that the *Every Evening* newspaper referred to Wilmington as "tributary to Philadelphia for its amusements."

13

By 1870 Wilmington was ready for a theatre. The city had matured as an industrial center, and a large percentage of its citizens had more leisure time. The growth of a new class of people who wanted reward and enjoyment in life was reflected in the increase of churches, fraternal groups, cultural societies, and social institutions.[10] Infected by the optimism which pervaded the entire country after the Civil War and before the Panic of 1873, Delaware leaders envisioned grandiose plans for Wilmington, and predicted it would undergo massive growth. By building a Wilmington Western railroad, they hoped to make Wilmington, already an important manufacturing center, into the metropolis of the East. In order to fulfill such a prophecy, Wilmington had to look like a big city. Building an opera house and a hotel were part of the attempt to transform Wilmington into a big city.[11] By 1850 the prejudice against theatre had lessened; theatre had become an honorable profession and a legitimate business enterprise;[12] therefore every cosmopolitan center needed a theatre. The architecturally superior Paris Opera House had become a model for Americans eager to embellish their cities.

Delaware was rescued from its theatreless state by the oldest fraternal organization in Delaware, the Most Worshipful Grand Lodge of Ancient Free and Accepted Masons. Freemasonry had a long tradition in Delaware: some of the early English settlers in Delaware were Masons; several lodges were formed during the 18th century. The Grand Lodge was duly constituted in 1806.[13] The Masonic order, a secular association which accepts members from monotheistic religions, is a system of ethics by which to guide one's life. Masons are concerned with improving the quality of life for all men; therefore charity plays a significant role in all degrees.[14]

As prominent citizens integrally involved in the improvement of Wilmington, the Masons recognized the need to furnish the city with a first class Opera House. Furthermore, the Masons needed a proper place to hold their meetings. During the first half of the 19th century, the Masons were continually on the move: from Old Town Hall to the College of Wilmington Building to Second & Shipley Streets to the Webb Building. As early as 1855, a joint meeting of all Delaware Masonic lodges was held to consider building a Temple, but no definite plans materialized until 1867 when the lodges met and agreed to construct a new Temple. Freemasonry is filled with mystery and ritual. One ritual dictates that Masons must meet

14

CIRCULAR!

The Undersigned, a Committee appointed by the different Lodges of this City, for the purpose of devising the best method by which a Masonic Hall can be erected, beg leave to submit to the Fraternity at large, the plan they have concluded upon.

They propose the formation of a Company under the name of the "**MASONIC HALL COMPANY,**" *with a capital of one hundred thousand dollars, ($100,000,) which they propose to divide into five thousand ($5,000) parts or shares, and fix the rate of each part or share at twenty dollars, ($20) to be paid in eight installments of two dollars and fifty cents ($2 50) each.   The first payment to be made immediately upon the organization of the Company, and the other every three months, dating from the organization.*

As soon as one-fourth of the Capital Stock shall be subscribed, there will be a meeting of the Stockholders for the Organization of the Company and election of a Board of Directors, (the number to be hereafter determined.)

Although no particular publicity has been given to the plan here proposed, it has met the hearty approval of all the Brethren, to whom it has been shown, and already quite a number of shares have been subscribed, (more than one-eighth of the whole number,) and we have every assurance that, in a few weeks after it shall be generally known, the whole amount will be taken.

The Committee beg leave further to state that this undertaking is one which will pay a good interest for the amount invested.   A building, such as is intended, is much needed by the public, and will command good rents for all such parts thereof as are intended for public use.   The parts devoted to the order, will yield a large return; and we do not hesitate to assert that the investment will pay seven per cent. (7.)   We therefore request that a fair consideration of the subject will be made by the Masonic Order, and those who desire to aid so worthy an undertaking, as the erection of a Temple dedicated to Charity.

The Committee will be pleased to furnish all information in their power.   Those desirous to subscribe to the Stock, (no matter how small the amount,) can address any of the Committee, at Wilmington, Delaware.

J. P. ALLMOND, Lodge No. 11,
J. H. SIMMS, M. D., Lodge No. 20,
R. HADDOCK, Lodge No. 20,   } *Committee.*
PHILEMMA CHANDLER, Lodge No. 1,
WILLIAM GRAVES, Lodge No. 14,
JOSHUA MARIS, Lodge No. 23.

in high places where guards can protect the privacy of the lodge. Since lodges could not meet on the ground floor, the area was devoted traditionally to commercial space or a public library or a theatre. Combining their own desire for a Temple with Wilmington's need for a theatre and their inability to use the ground floor for the Temple, the Masons planned to build a temple which would include a theatre and commercial space on the street level. Public notice of the new plan was given in a Circular, which stated the Masons' intention to build a "temple dedicated to charity" which would provide a building much needed by the public. In order to finance the temple, the Masons formed the Masonic Hall Company with capital of $100,000, composed of 5,000 shares to be sold to the general public at $20 a share.

ACT 1

❦

RISE TO GRANDEUR

SCENE ONE

SELECTION OF THE SITE

Subscriptions to the Masonic Hall Company sold well, and by the first meeting on March 22, 1869 one-half of the stock had been sold. George Lobdell was elected President; James Scott, Vice-President; John P. Allmond, Secretary; and Jesse Sharp, Treasurer.

One week after the elections, on March 31, the company appointed a committee to look for a site. The committee, composed of J. H. Simms, P. Chandler and J. Beggs, stated in their first report on May 13 that the Gordon lot, 100 feet on Market Street, running through to King Street, was available for $50,000. The lot, which was between Mr. Sharp's home at number 814 and the Misses Gordon at number 822, measured 92 feet on Market and went back 212 feet to King. Robert and Thomas Smith, who ran a marble and granite yard, were the prime tenants on the lot which also contained a great deal of building sand, a frame house, a brick house, and fencing.

The board agreed that the $50,000 price was too high and voted to offer the Gordons $30,000 for the lot. At the next meeting, President Lobdell reported that Mr. Dixon, an architect practicing in Baltimore, had recommended "the Masonic Hall Co. secure a plan before the lot was purchased and then make the purchase to suit the plan." Despite Mr. Dixon's recommendation, the committee continued to search for a site. The Chandler and Johnson hotel property at 5th and Market soon became a topic of discussion. The hotel property was an excellent location—on the same block as City Hall and adjacent to several hotels and banks. The Hall Co. actually made an offer for the property and was promised an answer in a week or 10 days. At this time, President Lobdell submitted a sketch for a 66 foot wide hall from Mr. Dixon.

Six months later, in December, the site question was still unresolved. The committee's first choice was the Chandler Johnson lot. The committee was instructed to buy the property at a price not to exceed $35,000 if it could be purchased with a clear title. If not, the committee was to buy the Gordon lot for not more than $35,000. When the site committee offered $27,000 for the Chandler Johnson property, it was informed the property was not on the market. (Ironically, the property was sold one year later and became the site of the Clayton House, one of Delaware's leading hotels.) However, the Gordon lot was still available and could be purchased at $36,800 for the entire 92 feet or at $400 per foot leaving at least 20 feet. The Hall Co. decided to offer the Gordons $300 a foot for the lot without specifying the number of feet.

During January 1870, the Hall Co. and the Gordon family negotiated the price of the lot. Finally on February 3, the Company agreed to the figure of $400 per foot and authorized President Lobdell to purchase the lot with a ten year mortgage on all but $1,000. The decision of whether to purchase 70 or 92 feet was postponed until the time of transfer since no design had been accepted.

But the Gordon family was a firm seller and would not accept the Masonic terms. The family insisted on $5,000 down payment when the articles of agreement were signed, another payment when the transfer was completed, and balance of funds in five years. Reaction among the Masonic Hall board was mixed. President Lobdell and building chairman Sharp were against closing the deal because they hoped for easier terms. But the majority of the board felt the lot had to be purchased at once because the company had secured many new subscriptions during the last week upon the representation that it had already purchased the lot. Mr. Lobdell reported to the board on February 26 that he had made a verbal agreement to purchase the lot from the Gordons. In order to secure substantial funds, installments were called in.

On March 31, 1870, exactly one year after the site committee had been formed, the Masonic Hall Co. drew an order of $5,000 to the Gordon heirs thereby finalizing the purchase of the lot. The Gordon lot was an excellent site in the expanding city. A horse railroad, which went up Market Street to 10th Street and then out Delaware Avenue to Rising Sun Avenue, was extending the city which formerly was centered at the waterfront. The imposing Wilmington Institute, an important meeting hall built in 1860-1861, was across the street on 8th and Market.[1] In 1876 numerous leading businesses lined Market Street, the business center of the city. Among the larger and more well known were: the local newspapers, *Delaware Gazette* and *Daily Commercial* on 4th and Market; the leading hotel, the Clayton House, the Delaware House and City Hall on 5th and

19

Market, the Bank of Delaware, Exchange Building and two insurance companies on 6th and Market, St. Paul's Church on 7th; the old school and First Presbyterian Church on 9th.[2] Although they had spent almost a year in choosing a site, the Masons had selected an important and central location for the city's new meeting hall.

View up Market Street from Second Street—an early center of Wilmington business because of its proximity to the waterfront

SCENE TWO

PREPARATION FOR CONSTRUCTION

No time was wasted; at the same March 31 meeting a committee on "Plans for Building" was appointed. The committee consisting of J. P. Allmond, James Beggs, T. M. Ogle, and President Lobdell, later became the building committee, which was the essential decision making body for the building. Although the board of the Hall Co. met weekly and heard reports, decisions were usually left to the discretion of the building committee.

Grace Methodist Church

In its first task, selecting an architect, the building committee did not begin in a void. Mr. Thomas Dixon had submitted a sketch nine months earlier in June 1869. Although he practiced in Baltimore, Mr. Dixon was well known to the Wilmington Masons since he was born in Wilmington, and had resided here until 1856. In 1865, after he moved to Baltimore, Mr. Dixon designed Grace Methodist Church, one of Wilmington's most architecturally significant buildings.

With the intention of attaining an outstanding architect, the committee extended its search to Philadelphia and New York. On April 11, the Committee on Plans reported that it had visited Philadelphia and called on several architects. Four architects had agreed to submit plans with the understanding that only the plan selected would be paid for. Given the advice of all architects who urged the committee to decide immediately whether to purchase 70 or 92 feet, the board voted to take the full 92 feet. Two weeks later, the committee reported a visit to several public halls in New York. Wallack's theatre appealed to the committee as "just the building we should use as a guide in architecture and furniture." Wallack's theatre was one of the most highly praised theatres in the country. Russell Smith, who was later our scenic designer, painted the proscenium of this famous playhouse.

At the July 12 meeting, the company discussed five plans submitted by Mr. Dixon of Baltimore, Mr. Sydney, Mr. Summers and Mr. Button of Philadelphia, and Mr. Ed Jeffries of Wilmington. Although the general arrangement of the building in all plans was similar and corresponded to the general direction given by the committee, Mr. Dixon's plan was considered preferable by the committee. Mr. Dixon was asked to come to Wilmington to make an estimate on the cost of constructing the hall "since the material used would be local." Mr. Dixon's estimate of $80,000 met with the committee's approval and he was hired as architect at the fee of $3,000, which would include superintending the building and paying his own traveling expenses.

When Thomas Dixon first moved to Baltimore he engaged in business for himself. In 1871 he was associated with Charles L. Carson, a young 24 year old. In later years, the prolific partnership of Dixon & Carson was responsible for the American Building, the Baltimore City Jail, Central Presbyterian Church and numerous others.[3] Charles Carson who was praised for his versatility, became one of Baltimore's leading architects.

In 1871, Mr. Dixon, the 53 year old senior partner, was in charge of the Opera House; decisions were usually made by him; all correspondence is signed by him. The younger Mr. Carson was responsible for most of the working drawings; he supervised the progress of the building and often came to Wilmington to make the monthly estimates.

More than a year had passed between the time Mr. Dixon submitted his original 1869 sketch and his final drawing. The primary difference between the two drawings is size. In 1869, the sketch was

Mount Vernon Place Methodist Episcopal Church, Baltimore, 1872,
by Thomas Dixon (AIA 1870) and Charles L. Carson (AIA, 1870)

23

for a hall sixty-six feet wide by eighty-six feet long and thirty-three feet high. At the time, Mr. Dixon boasted that it would be the largest hall in Wilmington, larger than Grace Methodist Church which was considered Wilmington's most monumental and fashionable building. The 1870 plan designed a much larger building, 91 feet by 132 feet. The 1869 sketch proposed one long end gallery and two side galleries; it mentioned the possibility of adding a second gallery. The final plan provided only one curved galley because Mr. Dixon had decided there was not enough height for a second gallery. Mr. Dixon's primary concern in 1869 was with the acoustics. He claimed the proportions were ideal for sound. In May of 1871 when Mr. Dixon was criticized for the floor level, he maintained that the floor level was proportioned to create the best line acoustically.

Dixon's plans, which were placed on display at Ziba Ferris, Jr. at 4th and Market, were praised by the community. The building was called a "splendid and imposing structure, a fine convention hall much better adapted to concerts than any the city now has.[4]

A Large Force

OF

ARTISTS,

EACH ONE A STAR,

Under the direction of Mr. Galbraith, all ready for the Spring Trade.

New and Beautiful Scenes

Above: Advertisement appearing in the March 12, 1872 issue of The Critique

Right: Montage of original bills from Grand Opera House contractors

24

Wilmington, Del., *February 8th 1872*

Masonic Hall co. For Stage.

$$\frac{352}{211\tfrac{1}{2}}\ \tfrac{6}{2}$$

To A. C. MITCHELL, Dr.

Jan	6	12½ days work	@ 125	46	63	
		1 lb. of clout nails	@ 17		17	
	9	332 ft. plank boards (for wing & flat) @ 5¾		19	6	21 70
	11	552 " " scenery style	@ 66	24	20	
		slipping " " 7¼ hrs	@ 35	5	09	
		" " 5 "	@ 25	2	75	
		2 pr. circular stop hinges			75	
		1 gro 1½ screws		1	47	
		35 ft. of boards	@ 5	1	75	293 14

Philadelphia, *April 12th* 1872.

M Wilmington Masonic Building Co.

To KEHRWIEDER BROTHERS, Dr.

DECORATIVE ARTISTS AND FRESCO PAINTERS,

(FROM THE DUSSELDORF ACADEMY,)

CO-OPERATIVE PRINT

No. 845 NORTH TENTH STREET.

for Fresco painting of
Ceiling and Walls etc. of
Theatre — $1800.00

Dec		By Stock	$500 =		
	16	" " Cash	600		00
1872		" "	300		
July 29		Cash	100		
April 13		Cash	150	1650 00	

Recd Payment in full 150.0
April 30th 1872 Kehrwieder Brothers

FOUNDRY, COR. SCOTT AND PRATT STS.   OFFICE, 24 LIGHT STREET.

Royer Bros.,

Builders' Iron Foundry

North-East cor. Ninth St. & Montgomery Avenue

Philadelphia, *Oct 6 1870*

J. P. Allmond Esq.,
of the first end.

In reply to yours
would state that we are
ready (at you convenience) to sign
Articles of agreement.

Respectfully

Thos. Dixon.   Chas. L. Carson.

DIXON & CARSON,

Architects,

117 WEST BALTIMORE STREET, CORNER SOUTH,

Baltimore, *Oct. 31.* 1871

J. P. Allmond, Esq.

Dear Sir.

Your letter of the 28"
reached our office to day when it was
too late for me to be in Wilm"
in time to make the estimate.
You may Expect me at the
building at 1. OCk. on Thursday
the 2. of Nov. for that purpose

Yours truly

Thos. Dixon.

PHILADELPHIA, *Dec. 18 1871*

Masonic Hall Co.
Wilmington Del.

BOUGHT OF CORNELIUS & SONS,

MANUFACTURERS OF GAS FIXTURES.

No. 821 CHERRY STREET.

TERMS:
Net Cash within 30 Days
from date of Shipment.

Forwarded per

9	5 lot. 6 hand. style #6581 Gilt $30		270 —
	2 ft. 4 in. long to order		
9	8 pr. to suit above Gilt $1		9 —
9	2 lot. 3 ft. style #6581 list $8		64 —
6	ft. Extra Pipe on 2 lot. Pend #6480 7/8		
6½	ft. " " 2 6 " Chand. #6370 1/2		
3	ft. " " 1 4 " 6370 1/2		
3 9/10	ft. " " 1 3 " 6480 1/8		
18	ft. " " 3 Rings 3/4 Gilt		
	No Charge sent pr. list lot.		
123	6½ in. Fch Rght. Glob.		
1	ft. lot. 3 ft. odd RX ft.		4 —
3	ft. 3/8 Cong. Pipe Gilt 1½ Bras		
	1 lot & 2 Boxes		4 55
			$357 55

Bids Under One Contract

John G. Haddock		H. F. Dure	
Wilmington	$92,469.10	Wilmington	$89,644.00
Jacob Jefferis		A. C. Mitchell	
Wilmington	$89,985.00	Wilmington	$90,954.00
P. H. Passmore Mitchell		Estrange Gould	
Wilmington	$88,500.00	Wilmington	$94,324.00
Philemma Chandler	$94,640.00		

Bids in 1870

Carpentry

E. Gould	$33,000.00
J. Jefferis	$31,300.00
John G. Haddock	$35,200.00
P. H. Mitchell	$32,784.00
H. F. Dure	$34,316.00
Amor Mitchell	$27,800.00

Millwork

Jackson and Sharpe	$ 5,350.00
Springer, Morley, Gause	$ 4,850.00

Brick Work

Perkins and Weldie	$19,546.00
Hizar and Lee	$20,826.00
Floyd and Brian	$22,643.00

Wrought Iron Work

Matsinger and Brothers Philadelphia	$ 1,923.66
Davison, Haven, Heuvelman, New York	$ 1,930.00
Bartlett and Robbins Baltimore	$ 1,610.00
David Woolman Wilmington	$ 1,285.75

Cast Iron

Bartlett and Robbins	$21,558.00
Davison, Haven, Heuvelman, New York	$18,095.00
Samuel J. Creswell Philadelphia	$18,000.00
Samuel J. Bailey Philadelphia	$
Royer Brothers Philadelphia	$16,810.00

Tin Work

R. Morrison	$ 2,562.00
H. F. Pickels	$ 1,873.48
George Dorsey	$ 2,299.00

Masonry Work and Granite

Robert Scott	$ 2,666.00

Masons and Excavating

Washington Cox	$ 2,650.00

Excavating

Thomas Ford	$.30 per cubic yard

Plumbing and Gasfitting

Gawthrop and Brothers	$ 2,225.00

The Building Committee accepted the following bids, as announced in the *Wilmington Daily Commercial,* October 24, 1871.

A. C. Mitchell	$27,800.00
Perkins and Weldie Brick, Stone	$19,546.00
Perkins and Weldie Plastering	$ 6,186.00
James France Painting, Glazing	$ 4,646.00
David Woolman Wrought Iron Work	$ 1,285.00
Royer Brothers Cast Iron	$16,910.00
H. F. Pickels and Brothers, Tin Work	$ 1,873.48
Gawthrop and Brothers Plumbing, Gas Fitting	$ 2,225.00

Bids in 1871

Frescoing

Lankan and Ksenyer (Plus $200 Design)	$ 1,350.00
Mohr and Lanbeck	$ 1,200.00
Herman T. Fuchs	$ 1,500.00
Kehrwieder	$ 1,800.00

Upholstery

Murphy and Brothers	$1.60 each
Noble, Brown	
George C. Macan	$1.40 and $1.15 each, then reduced 10%

Roof Slate

A. C. Mitchell	$265 for slate and felt
Jacob Hensel	$384 for Lehigh slate and felt
Gault	$250

Heating

Gawthrop and Brothers	$ 8,500.00
Wister and Botton	$ 8,975.00
Pancoast and Maul	$ 6,832.50
John McConn	$ 5,975.00

Scenery

Mr. Love	$ 7,000.00
Russell Smith	$ 2,300.00

The building committee began advertising for "proposals for constructing the temple under one contract and for the several parts separately" in early September. All proposals were to be delivered sealed to the committee by September 29 at three PM.

The advertisements caused good response. Seven Wilmington contractors bid on the whole job. Bids ranged from a low of $88,500 from Passamore H. Mitchell to a high of $94,640 from P. Chandler. [See complete listing] The Company also received numerous bids for separate portions. The largest number of bids for any single item was received for carpentry. Six of the firms that had bid as general contractors also bid on the carpentry job. On most items, the bids were from Wilmington firms; yet cast-iron was a speciality which attracted national attention. Of the five bids for cast-iron, three were from Philadelphia firms, one from New York and one from Baltimore.

When the Masonic Hall Co. convened to discuss the bids, on September 30, it discovered that there was a difference of $7,176.90 between the lowest price for the whole building, $88,500, and the lowest price for the individual portions added together, $81,323.10. The difference was attributed to the risk factor incurred by one contractor's assuming full responsibility. In the interest of saving money, the Masonic Hall Co. opted to accept the lowest bids for individual estimates. The decision was to have long range implications because by contracting in this fashion, the Hall Co. assumed definite responsibilities. When a feud arose over the number of iron braces the smith had to supply, Mr. Dixon reminded the company that since it had signed separate contracts, it was responsible for all contingency fees.

The seven contractors with the lowest bids were announced in the newspaper on October 24, 1870. The group included six Wilmington contractors and a cast iron firm from Philadelphia. The total work contracted, $80,471.48, was very close to Dixon's original $80,000 estimate. However, the total did not include heating, seating, gas fixtures, scenery, frescoing or slate work, all of which were contracted one year later in October and November, 1871 and added another $16,525, exclusive of Cornelius's light fixtures which cost at least $750. Curiously, most of the contracts signed in 1871 for specialized interior work were to non-Wilmington firms. The total cost of the building at the time of its completion was approximately $97,700.

The articles of agreement between the Masonic Hall Co. and all contractors, which were signed on October 14, 1870, carefully delineated the responsibility of each. According to the payment terms, each was to be paid on a monthly basis between the first and fifth of the month after Mr. Dixon estimated the amount of work done. Payments would be for 80% of the cost; the remainder would be paid on completion of the total job. A deadline for the completion of work was given, and need to work with dispatch was emphasized.

The carpenter, Amor Mitchell, was also hired as foreman of the job for an additional $1,500. As Mr. Dixon explained, "Mr. Mitchell should be held responsible for all dimensions: he receives instructions from us and in our absence communicates with the different parties in the building."

By the end of October the design was finalized, all work was contracted, and everything was ready except the lot. The agreement with the Gordon family gave the Company possession of the lot as of January 1, 1871. All of the tenants on the lot were willing to move sooner, but the Smith brothers, operators of the marble yard, would not vacate before December unless the company lent them $1,000. On December 29, the Hall Co. completed the sale of land with a payment of $3,800. The frame and brick buildings on the property were sold by Ogle and Miller at public auction on December 31 for $125.00. By the beginning of January, construction began.

SCENE THREE

MONTHLY PROGRESS OF THE CONSTRUCTION

Winter

During January, February, and early March preliminary work began: the site was excavated, the foundation was dug, lumber ordered in November was delivered. According to the specifications, all joists, girders, and rafters were cut by January 1 and carpentry was begun. By early April, carpentry work not on the grounds was insured for $1,500.

28

During the early months, while reviewing Dixon's plans, the committee made serious enquiries. In early January the committee proposed a change in the roof trusses. Mr. Dixon informed the committee that he did like the proposed alterations to the roof trusses because "to take out the diagonal rods will weaken the trusses. Iron braces would add strength to the building but are unnecessary." A few weeks later the committee was challenging the stone foundation walls. Mr. Dixon defended the walls saying "we are well satisfied that the stone walls are thick enough. The wall is 23 inches thick with a 21 inch thick brick wall—this is correct."

Spring

From March to July all work concerned the basic structural shell: completing the excavation, digging the foundation, building foundation walls, brick walls, wood frames, and installing wrought iron supports.

In March, while Perkins and Weldie were digging the foundation, they discovered that the northeast foundation was too soft. Mr. Dixon insisted the foundation be dug down to solid bottom. Perkins and Weldie dug through the clay to reach a solid foundation, but later increased their bill accordingly. The inevitable conflict between Perkins and Weldie and the Masonic Hall Co. was finally resolved with a compromise when Mr. Dixon explained in July that Perkins and Weldie were obliged by contract to go deep enough to get a good foundation but when they went below clay to get a uniform foundation as you requested, the company was responsible." Once the excavation was complete, Perkins and Weldie began laying granite slabs for the foundation.

When the foundation walls were being built during April they excited a great deal of public criticism, as the January letter had anticipated. Mr. Dixon rejected adamantly the idea that the walls were too thin and claimed such an opinion was invalid in a letter of April 17, 1871:

For my own part, as architect of the building, I would not heed such talk, as it is usually indulged in by those whose judgment in such matters is not very accurate, a mere expression of opinion that cannot be sustained by reason or the echo of such an opinion prompted perhaps by a mean spirit of jealousy or by a foolish ambition to seem wise.

By April 20 the stone foundation walls were complete and "everything was in readiness for laying the cornerstone." The cornerstone ceremony was a festive occasion, although it began two hours late because of a rain storm. A procession, led by Chief Marshal Thomas Ogle, Masonic leaders, the Masonic officers, and architect Dixon, marched from Front Street up Market Street to 16th Street then over to King Street and to the temple site where a platform had been erected for the occasion. After a short ceremony, the cornerstone was laid at the northeast corner of the structure in accordance with Masonic ritual.[5]

Perkins and Weldie, who were now referred to as bricklayers, began constructing the exterior walls in May and worked through June and July. They were paid $3,600, $3,850, and $2,000 for each of these months. Although the building committee announced at the end of May that "everything was progressing finely," the job did run into unforeseen problems resulting in great delay. According to the original arrangement, the brick work was to be finished ready for roof timbers by July, and Amor Mitchell was to have the roof timbers up by the end of the month. In actuality, some of the brick work was not finished until November, thereby throwing Mitchell into short days for all his work. The delay presented such a problem that in October 1872 he sued the company for $1,500.

While the exterior brick walls were under construction, the building committee continued to re-examine the plans and drawings. The committee questioned the idea of putting a second gallery in the theatre, but Mr. Dixon stated there was not sufficient height and the iron columns would have to be increased in strength to carry the weight of a second gallery. Mr. Dixon also defended the level of the parquet floor; "we think it is right according to the *acoustical line* that should govern in such matters. The parquet floor is level about two-thirds of the way and then begins to rise."

During August and September the basic shell was completed. By the end of September the building was roofed in, but Gault and Son did not slate the roof until mid-November.

Fall

By early October the girder of the gallery was in place and the main stairways were installed. At this time the board met in the

30

theatre of the temple to discuss two problems. The first and primary issue was the level of the parquet floor which had been discussed in the spring and was to become the major problem over the years. Mr. Beggs, chairman of the building committee, stated that the parquet floor was entirely too flat to get a good view of the stage. After careful deliberation the board decided the sight problem could be remedied by lowering the footlights. Despite the committee's opinion Mr. Dixon stood firm in his opinion that the stage and parquet floor were correct.

The second issue involved the alleged negligence of a contractor. Water was dripping down the walls to the foundation and the walls were wet because H. F. Pickels, the tin work contractor, had neglected to put in conductors to carry water from the building. Mr. Pickels was informed he must put them in at once and deduct the cost from his contract.

By mid-October, the gallery floor was being laid. On October 25, the plastering was underway. The *Every Evening* reported "the whole interior is a wilderness of scaffolding."

Three of the four exterior walls were brick but the Market Street façade was a handsome cast-iron structure. Although the contract had been awarded to Royer Brothers of Philadelphia in October 1870, the firm did not receive working drawings until the spring. The first large portion of the façade was set in August. About one-half of the total estimate was paid at this time. Another large portion was completed in October. By early November, when the work was not complete, the Hall Co. sent a warning letter to Royer Brothers. Their indignant response was that they had not held up work, but could not set the hyatt lights on the store doors until the stone pavement was in place. Substantial payments to Royer Brothers in February, March, and May demonstrate that work on the façade continued well into 1872. Despite the fact that it was incomplete, by mid-November the façade was painted white.

The three niches on the façade were originally supposed to contain statutes of Faith, Hope, and Charity. In July President Lobdell saw a beautiful statue at Bailey and Company in Philadelphia and suggested contacting them. In August Mr. Dixon recommended contacting James and Kirtland in New York, who sent an estimate of $360 for each figure. By early September, the building committee was authorized to purchase the statues at $360 each. Suddenly the modeler changed his price and James and Kirtland were forced to renege. In December 1873, in the annual report to stockholders, President Lobdell reported the committee could not secure the statues at the correct price.

Although various committees had been organized during the summer to consider heating, scenery, lighting, seating, and other interior details, no contracts were signed until October 15, a mere two months before the scheduled opening of December 22, 1871. Some contracts—frescoing, scenery—were not finalized until November. The speed with which the decisions and work were made is incredible.

Lighting

Given their meticulous care in following the building process, the building committee was able to change and improve the original lighting system. Dixon's original plan included a large, central gas light chandelier. In August 1871 President Lobdell warned the board that "I fear we have not adopted the best lighting arrangement." He cited the recommendation of a Mr. Elliott of the Philadelphia Academy of Music who advised using an electrical apparatus which was to be installed in the Philadelphia Academy of Music and would pay for itself in a short time by the gas that would be saved by lighting all the lights simultaneously. President Lobdell also claimed that St. James Hall in Buffalo, which used no chandeliers, was the best and most economically lit hall he knew. He suggested using side lights with reflectors instead of chandeliers in order to give better light.

Although the idea of lighting the theatre without chandeliers was not accepted, lighting continued to be a major issue. On October 6 a Mr. Stratton of Philadelphia proposed a new mode of lighting entirely different than the one proposed by Mr. Dixon. Mr. Stratton's plan eliminated the central chandelier and instead supplied light from light brackets around the gallery and from three small chandeliers over the gallery. Stratton's proposal was cheaper because it omitted the expensive center chandelier. Furthermore, by putting the three chandeliers on a separate supply line so that they had no connection with brackets on side walls, they could be turned totally off and insure a more perfectly dark scene. In October the board adopted Mr. Stratton's proposal, and Gawtrop and Brothers

32

began making the necessary changes in the gas pipes. Stratton and Brothers did gas fittings for the stage, the footlights, border lights, installed footlights around the stage, and the lamp posts outside the hall. Chandeliers were ordered from Cornelius & Sons.

When the theatre opened it was lit by three clusters of gas lights from the ceiling, nine clusters of chandeliers (each of five lights) from the front of the gallery, and from brackets extending from the side walls both above and below the gallery.[6]

Heating

In late June, as soon as the basic shell seemed under control, the heating committee was appointed. The committee spent the summer and early fall interviewing various companies. On October 15, 1871 the Company signed a contract with Gawthrop and Brothers (the same company that had been contracted for the gas and plumbing in 1870) for $8,500 to heat the building. Their work performed in November and December included installing a boiler under King Street. The steam heating of the building was praised. For summer ventilating, a large ventilator was installed in the center of the ceiling over the auditorium.

Scenery

In early July a committee on flats and scenery was appointed and began interviewing numerous artisans. Early in the fall the committee contracted Russell Smith of Philadelphia. A long letter of October 9, 1871 from Mr. Smith states that he could do the work described by the Hall Co. as:

I have the conveniences here for the execution of such work, where I paint scenes and curtains for the principal theatres in Boston, New York and Philadelphia.

He then claimed he was unable to give an estimate until he knew the size of the scenes, wings and curtains as well as the number needed. Apparently the Hall Co. was still uncertain how much scenery was needed, and Mr. Smith answered their quandry in this same letter:

. . . as to the number of scenes, the means you have and object or kind of performances you have in view, must be your guide. Ten scenes and about 40 wings would be about as small a stock as you could perform with, and 20 scenes with 60 wings would be a full supply.

The committee pursued other artists, and on October 15 it was on the verge of signing a $7,000 contract with Mr. Love of Philadelphia, whose studio they planned to visit.

Imagine the delight of the committee when it received Mr. Smith's letter of October 26 with an estimate of $2,000 for the 10 scenes, 40 wings, 1 arch drapery, 1 straight drapery, 2 tormentors and 3 sky borders:

this is the lowest price at which I can undertake it; and if it should seem high to you, it is because the list is the choice stock of a theatre; every scene requiring much more labor or time and care than those used for occasional pieces.

His proposal was accepted immediately, but the contract price was $2,300 since it included a painted drop curtain for an additional $300.

By hiring Mr. Smith the Hall Co. was securing one of the outstanding scenic and landscape artists in the country. In 1857, while reporting on the opening of the Academy of Music in Philadelphia, the *New York Tribune* reported:

the beauty of the scenery attracted the most admiration. Such landscapes as were presented by Russell Smith have never before been seen in this country.[7]

According to his biographer, Virginia Lewis, Mr. Smith used a distemper technique, a water glue solution which he made in his own shop. Mr. Smith believed that color should reflect the beauty of Nature, and he strongly objected to the "fictitious or artificial palette characteristic of inadequate scene painters." His method of working was painstaking and included a sketch in pencil and a preliminary painting before the final scene or curtain.

When Mr. Smith offered his estimate, he realized that time was a major problem and wrote in an October 25 letter:

thinking it possible that you may require me to do the work, and as it would be of the utmost consequence to save time, I have taken a canvas I had sewed for the Academy of Music . . . and shall begin upon it tomorrow.

By working at his utmost speed, Mr. Smith completed a large portion of the contract, including the garden, prison, kitchen chamber, and several wings, by December 18. The sets were sent by railroad because the river had frozen and boats had stopped running.

The stage had been arranged for scenery by Mr. Charles Higbee, a Philadelphia carpenter responsible for the stage at the Academy of Music. The sets arrived and were installed immediately; the drop curtain was also hung. At the opening, the drop curtain and sets received great praise. The remaining scenery was sent on January 3 and Mr. Smith claimed in a letter of January 3, 1872: "we were all very flad . . . for we never have before pushed so hard to complete a contract . . ."

The Hall Co. was well pleased with the sets and paid $1,000 immediately. In mid-February Mr. Smith suggested that, although he felt some delicacy about advising the Masonic Hall Co. to purchase additional scenery, he felt the theatre needed a landscape scene. The company immediately accepted his advice, and ten days later Mr. Smith sent woods, trees, and landscape. He advised that the new set should be used with lights behind it to avoid shadows.

The happy relationship between Mr. Smith and the Company is epitomized by a note from Mr. Smith when he received final payment in March:

I would not be doing you and yours justice if I were to close this note without adding that in all my business intercourse with managers and other men, I have never been quite so handsomely treated as by you gentlemen . . .

Seating

Although the building committee was not authorized to make arrangements concerning the seating of the theatre until September, seating was a concern during the summer. In August Mr. Dixon recommended that the committee see the seats "of the new Opera House style" which Bartlett and Robbins had furnished for the Holiday Street Theatre and Ford's Theatre in Baltimore. On November 1 the committee did contract with Bartlett and Robbins for 250 cast-iron seats, ready for upholstery at $2.75 each. A sample chair arrived on November 11. The frames of the chair were cast-iron; the seat flew up against the back to make more room between rows. On December 11 Mr. Dixon notified the company that the chairs had been shipped, for which he was preparing seating diagrams including a central parquet section, a horseshoe shaped parquet, and a gallery. On December 15 Bartlett and Robbins sent up two men to install the chairs into the floor. After the chairs were installed, the Company ordered 18 more. On November 1 the Company also arranged for the remaining 1,141 seats to be made by Amor Mitchell of solid wood for $1.25. Mr. Mitchell worked with amazing speed, and, by the end of November, the solid walnut chairs were being installed in the parquet circle.

The company received several bids for upholstery, and, on November 1, it accepted the bid of Mr. George Macan. According to the contract, Mr. Macan would use patent elastic felt and enamel drill to upholster the seats and backs of the parquet chairs for $1.26 each and the seats of the wood chairs for $1.03½. Although the seating contracts were finalized only in November, all the seats were in place and upholstered by the time of the opening.

Ceiling

The frescoed ceiling was designed to be the crowning glory of the theatre. The company received bids from two Baltimore firms and two Philadelphia firms. One of the bidders, Herman T. Fuchs of Fuchs and Kumms, sent numerous letters of recommendation with his estimate of $1,500. He explained that he considered the job "an opportunity to establish a good reputation outside of Philadelphia, which is my sole object in estimating for it."

However, the firm of Kehrwieder Brothers, Decorative Artists and Fresco Painters, sustained the interest of the Masonic Hall Company. At the end of September, Mr. Kehrwieder wrote to Mr. Allmond stating that he had been to see Mr. Dixon in Baltimore and would get back to the promised design at once. On October 11 the firm sent a proposal to "paint and decorate the ceiling and main auditorium with groups of figures and ornamental work after a design furnished by us and expressly drawn for the purpose of the work." The work would be done for $1,800 plus $200 for the design. The final articles of agreement were not actually signed until November 6—very close to the opening date of December 22. According to the contract, work was to be finished in four weeks from the time the ceiling was ready. By November 28 the *Every Evening* reported that "the frescoers are working on the ceiling." On December 13, they reported; "the fresco painters are adding finishing touches to the ceiling and have begun painting the walls." Finishing the ceiling in so short a time was most difficult. On December 19 the

Delaware Gazette reported: "The Kehrwieder Brothers of Philadelphia have worked from early morn till 10 o'clock at night with seventeen men for ten days to finish the ceiling."

Winter

The progress of the construction became a matter of great community interest and the newspapers often carried progress reports. During November and December the theatre was the scene of constant activity.[8] Gas fitters, frescoers, painters, carpenters and upholsterers worked long hours together. Miraculously, the theatre was completed in time for the December 22 opening, although work on the remainder of the building continued for several months. Some of the upper stories were available for tenants in March; the four main floor stores were not ready until the fall.

Enlargement of illustration appearing on early stationery

SCENE FOUR

SPLENDID NEW ORNAMENT ON MARKET STREET

The imposing Masonic Temple, 211 feet by 92 feet, with its "richly ornate front" completely overshadowed the adjacent houses "which in their insignificance reached only to the third of the four story [78 feet high] giant." [9]

The ornate façade, made entirely of finely finished cast-iron from the sills and risers of the doors to the cornice, was painted

38

white in imitation of chiseled marble. Modelled after the famous
Paris Opera House, and built in the French Second Empire style,
the temple was distinctly American in its use of cast-iron. Cast-iron
architecture became increasingly popular during the 19th century
because while cast-iron simulated stone, it could be produced more
rapidly and economically.[10] The rich vermiculation on the columns,
reminescent of Mannerist stone work, and the variation of the column capitols depended upon the decorative capacities of cast-iron.
Furthermore, since cast-iron is strong in compression, a small
amount can support great weight. The street level, composed of four
stores each of three cast-iron arches, contained large sheet glass
windows which were decoratively handsome as well as commercially
advantageous.

Since the "splendid new ornament on Market Street"[11] was
primarily a Masonic Temple, the design of the façade incorporated
important Masonic principles. In its complex symbolism, Freemasonry relies heavily on odd numbers, particularly the numbers,
3, 5, and 7. There are 3 principal officers in a lodge, 3 degrees of
Masonry: apprentice, fellowcraft and master masons, and 3 grand
pillars which support Masonry: knowledge, strength and beauty.
A man passes through 3 stages of life: youth, manhood and age.
Five is a sacred and mystical number symbolic of life as it is lived,
of happiness and misery, birth and death, order and disorder. There
are 5 orders of architecture and 5 human senses. Seven, the most
potent number in ancient religions, is significant in Masonic thought.
There are 7 steps in the Winding Stairs; 7 men are needed to open an
Entered Apprentice lodge.[12]

The symmetrical design of the façade was based on these numbers. The façade was divided in 5 basic sections. The center section
became number 3 when the sections were counted from left to center
or from right to center. On the storefront level, each store comprised
3 sections. The entrance to the building (the central arch) became
the 7th arch when one counted from left or right to center. There
were 5 doors on the ground level. On the second and third floors,
each of the 5 sections included 3 arches and 3 keystones. On the
Mansard roof, the windows were set in groups of 3, 2, 2, 2, 3 so that
there were 7 windows when counted from left or right to center.
From the street level to the top of the Mansard roof, there were 5
levels—3 stories, a mansard roof and a cupola level.

Freemasonry is veiled in allegory and illustrated by symbol. Several Masonic symbols were displayed prominently on the façade. A large *"G"* symbolizing God and Geometry was in the middle of the central arch on the third level. Just above the *G,* in the central pediment, stood the all seeing eye, one of the oldest and most widespread symbols denoting God. Large cast-iron letters, A F & A M, on the second level central section referred to the full name of the order—Ancient Free and Accepted Masons.

The elaborate Mansard roof covered with slate was crowned with three ornamental towers, around each of which stood an iron railing 2½ feet high. A flag staff 35 feet high was mounted on the middle tower. Two ornamental lamps lettered with the words Masonic Temple stood in front of the hall.

The rear of the building (the King Street side) was faced with good Press Brick. Each of the side brick walls contained fourteen windows, seven on each level. The roof was tin.

One entered the building by passing under a central cast-iron arch and through folding wooden doors with heavy moldings. The narrow lobby (16½ feet wide) was lit by two 6-light chandeliers at the ticket booth, on the immediate right. At the end of the lobby were three entrances to the parquet and two stairways to the gallery.

The auditorium (133 feet in length, 75 feet in width, and some 42 feet in height) was praised by all local newspapers as one of the most handsome theatres in the United States and among the best adapted for stage performances and acoustics. The large (45 feet by 75 feet) stage was covered with a specially woven carpet and was trimmed with footlights and border lights. In the center of the stage was a trap door from "whence came the ghosts" so popular in Victorian drama. On either side of the stage were two columns in imitation of scagliola with gilt caps. A gilt carved eagle with outstretched wings ornamented the top of the decorative proscenium arch. An upper and lower proscenium box, trimmed with Nottingham lace, stood on either side of the stage. Russell Smith's handpainted curtain dominating the area was described in detail by every newspaper.

Right: Masonic diploma of Jacob DeWolf, an influential businessman who ran a clothing store on Market Street after the Civil War and was an energetic organizer of the Wilmington Jewish community

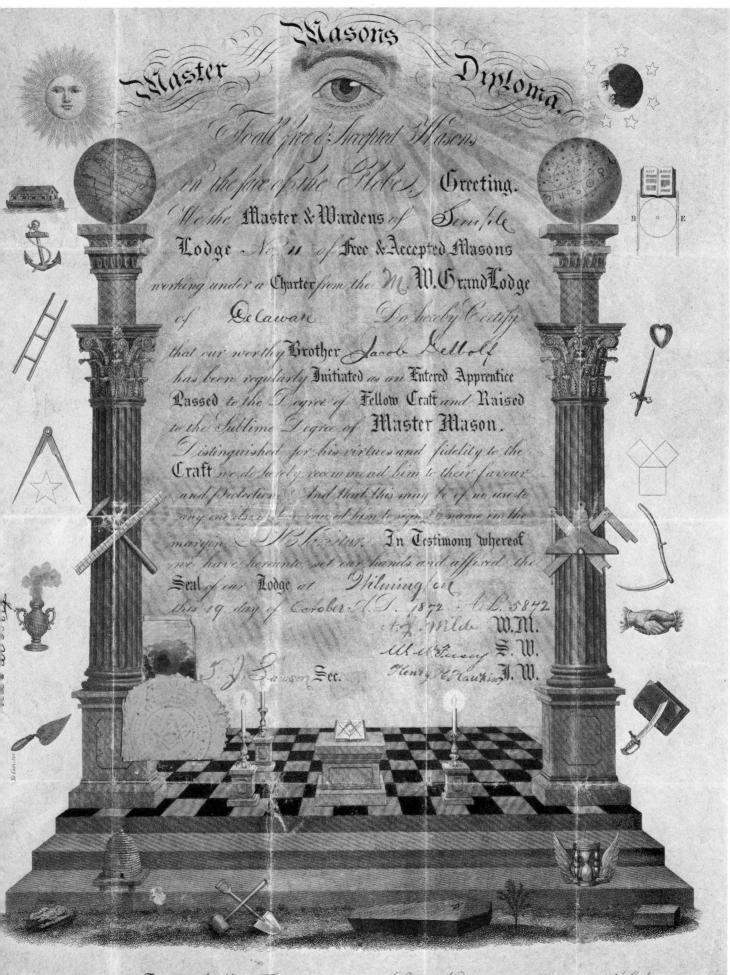

The description in the *Delaware Republican* explained:

The drop curtain is twenty-eight feet high, by forty feet wide, and is one of the handsomest in the entire country. It represents an Italian City on the borders of a lake, which is spanned by a stone bridge, surrounded by hills and glistening in the golden rays of the setting sun, while a large vessel is sailing up the lake, on the opposite side is a small skiff, from which a man is stepping ashore. Heavy stone steps lead down the hill to the water's edge, and end in an abutment built in an artistic and ornamental style. One of the most prominent features is a large tree under which three goats are browsing under the tender herbage.

The theatre was divided into three major seating areas: a horseshoe-shaped central parquet, a surrounding parquet circle, and a gallery or balcony. Although the total seating capacity varies slightly according to accounts, the general distribution of seats is clear.[13] There were approximately 924 seats downstairs; 24 box seats; 255-

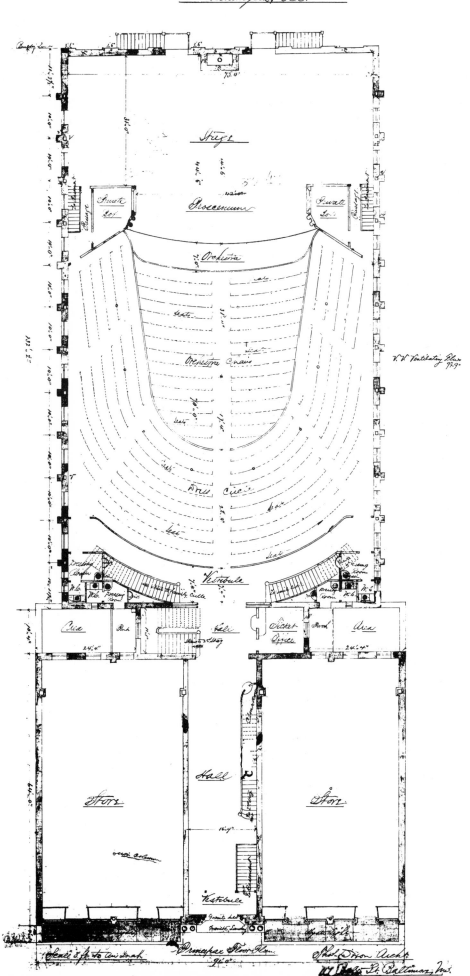

Design for Masonic Hall
Wilmington, Del.

275 parquet seats and the remainder in the parquet circle; and 500 seats in the gallery. Given the strength of cast-iron, eight slender cast-iron columns supported the weight of the large balcony, which was admirably constructed to provide good sight and acoustical lines from the farthest seat. The graceful curve of the delicate looking balcony reflected the shape of the cast-iron arches of the façade. The entire balustrade of the balcony was cast-iron, painted white with red and gold ornamentation.

The patent iron chairs, cast by Bartlett and Robbins, stood in the parquet. Their tilting seats, still an innovation in 1871, rendered passage to one's seat easier. The seats and backs of the cast-iron frame chairs were upholstered in maroon enamel drill, a simulated leather. The remaining seats in the parquet circle and balcony were Amor Mitchell's wood chairs. Only the seats of these chairs were upholstered with the same enamel drill.

The magnificent frescoed ceiling was the "crowning glory." Architect Thomas Dixon, who was continually concerned with the theatre's acoustics, wisely designed a flat ceiling without curves to trap the flow of sound. However, the ceiling was made to look like a dome by using a central small circle of cerulean blue and a larger outer circle:

In the centre is a field of blue ornamented with gilt stars and surrounding this is a larger paneled circle containing representations of the muses who are to preside over the varied entertainments of which the new opera house is to be the scene. In the front group are Melpomene and Thalia, Goddesses of Tragedy and Comedy; on the right hand are Calliope, Goddess of Epic Poetry and Polypuian, Goddess of Rhetoric; on the left stand Urania, Patroness of Astronomy and Cilo, Muse of History whilst toward the main entrance are grouped Erato and Terpsichore . . .[14]

The house was lit by three gas jets hanging from the ceiling; nine cast-iron chandeliers each composed of five lights hanging from the balcony balustrade; and brackets extending from the walls both above and below the gallery. The theatre was decorated with Victorian lavishness—the walls were handsomely frescoed in panels of bright crimson or chocolate brown (descriptions vary). The coping around the boxes, parquet, and gallery were trimmed with plush. There were two star dressing rooms and six dressing rooms in the basement.

44

The auditorium committee had spared neither pains nor expense, and the public was fully appreciative of the outstanding result. "No city of Wilmington's size can boast a more commodious opera house or theatre than this, and none of any size a more beautiful one" commented the *Every Evening* after opening night.

Interest in renting the new hall for opening night had been widespread well before the theatre opened. As early as February 1871, while the foundation of the building was being dug, the Diamond State Guards wrote to the Masons requesting the hall for an opening night ball. But the Masons were unwilling to make a commitment ten months early. A few months later another local group, the Grand Army of the Republic, attempted to secure the hall for the two opening weeks and received a similar reply.

By the fall, interest in renting the theatre had spread to a national level. In September Mr. Elliott of the Academy of Music wrote to request the opening night for a first class opera. He promised to "bring something very fine—to establish the house." Mr. Elliott was refused because by this time, the Masons had decided to reserve opening night for a ball. In November Mr. J. T. Ford, manager of the Grand Opera House and the Holiday Street theatre in Baltimore, was granted use of the theatre for the opening week.

In December reports on the magnificent new structure were accompanied by enthusiastic expectations: "This introduction of legitimate drama to our midst will be an event of importance to our pleasure-seeking citizens that will ultimately end in supplying our people here at home with that necessary and instructive amusement." [14]

THE CRITIQUE.

VOL. I.   WILMINGTON, DEL., MARCH 12, 1872.   No. 12

VOL. IV. No. 24   WEDNESDAY EVENING, NOVEMBER 15th, 1882.   J. F. SPECK, PUBLISHER AND PRINTER.

VOL. 3. No. 56.   WILMINGTON, DEL., JANUARY 24, 1882.   FERRIS BROS., PUBLISHERS AND PRINTERS.

VOL. VI.   WEEK ENDING MARCH 16, 1895.   No. 138.

Montage of mastheads from nineteenth century programs of
The Grand Opera House

ACT 2

&

GRAND YEARS
OF
THE GRAND
1871-1910

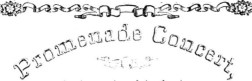

Promenade Concert,

On the occasion of the Opening
OF

THE MASONIC TEMPLE,

Wilmington, Delaware,

Friday Eve, Dec. 22d, 1871.

Programme

FOR

Concert.

No. 1.—*Selections from Balfe's Opera.*

Puritan's Daughter.

No. 2.—*Rage of America,*

Serio-Comic Fantasia, Kingleien.

No. 3.—*Amazon Galop.*

Faust.

No. 4.—*Aria, from the opera of Ernani*

No. 5.—*Sweet Spirit hear my Prayer,*

McClurg.

No. 6.—*Genevieve de Brabant,*

Offenbach.

No. 7.—*Aria, from the opera of Pelisar,*

Backjard.

No. 8.—*Selections : We have met, loved, and parted.*

McClurg.

Committee of Arrangements.

WM. H. JAMAR,	ISAAC C. PYLE,
JAS. CROSBY,	JAS. CROOKS,
D. R. HAYES,	J. T. MYNICH,
J. H. CAMERON,	A. WILLISCROFT,
W. S. HOLDEN,	J. V. CHRISTY,
W. T. MARSHALL,	H. B. M'INTIRE.

Director, - - WILLIAM H. JAMAR.

Floor Managers.

ALFRED GAWTHROP,	THOS. HOLT,
WM. O. HAYS,	WM. T. SPRINGER,
JAS. CROOKS,	SAM'L KEMP,
JAS. CROSBY,	WM. W. FUREY,
FRANK S. DANGEL,	COL. E. R. HEISLER,
JAS. HAWKINS,	WM. P. SMITH,

MUSIC

Especially arranged for the Occasion

BY

McClurg's Orchestra.

REFRESHMENTS

Served in Banquet Room,

From 11 to 3 o'clock.

GEO. H. ROBINSON, *Restaurateur.*

SCENE ONE

OPENING SEASON

The opening of the Opera House was "the event of the decade in the history of amusements in Wilmington." As the *Wilmington Daily Commercial* commented: "at last Wilmington has a first class Opera House and can command the visits of first class dramatic companies."[1] The grand opening, a promenade concert and ball held on December 22, was "an affair far ahead of anything of this character ever before attempted." The concert was not limited to the Masonic fraternity; tickets were available to the entire community. By opening evening, curiosity about the interior was so intense that people commenced dropping in by 8 o'clock, and "by 9 o'clock the gallery and parquet circle were pretty fairly filled. In one sense very fairly, since many of Wilmington's fairest daughters lent their smiles to brighten the occasion and quite a number of beautiful and stylish ladies were there from other cities."[2]

The evening began at precisely 9 o'clock when McClurg's orchestra which was positioned in the extreme left of the dress circle, struck up a march and a promenade led by Colonel B. R. Heisler and Miss Zilpha Edwards of Philadelphia marched down the center aisle. A musical programme of some eight selections lasted until 11 o'clock. Trumpeters then called the dancers to the floor and the patrons danced for several hours. The dance was criticized for the large number of quadrilles and the absence of the gallop. In the wee hours of the morning refreshments were served in a temporary banquet room on the first floor. The affair was considered "one of the most brilliant and successful of any ever witnessed in our city."

But the real dedication of the new Opera House "to the purpose for which it was built" was held on Christmas day at 2 o'clock when the Wallack-Richings Combination Co. presented *Daisy Farm,* the first of eight Christmas week performances. "The house was crowded from pit to dome, every seat being taken and all available

Left: Pages of a booklet distributed at the promenade concert and ball

49

THE CRITIQUE.

VOL. I. WILMINGTON, DEL., MARCH 12, 1872. No. 12

The jealousy between the songstresses Lucca and Mallinger was publicly manifested on the Berlin Royal Opera stage one evening recently. The "Marriage of Figaro" was being performed, and the two prima donnas and their partisans grew more and more warlike from act to act, until it became impossible to proceed. Lucca then stepped forward and scolded the audience bitterly for applauding and hissing, while Mallinger sat down and burst into tears. At last quiet was restored, but the altercation was renewed outside the house, and the Emperor was obliged to order the street to be cleared,

———:o:———

Adelina Patti, now the Marchioness deCaux, used to run about barefoot in New York. Rubini, the tenor, was a journeyman tailor. Watchel drove a cab in Hamburg, and many a tenor he took to the opera house before he got into it himself.

———:o:———

" Boy, why did you take an armful of my shingles on Sunday?" "Why, Sir, mother wanted some kindling wood, and I didn't want to split wood on Sunday."

———:o:———

Car stops; smiling young lady enters; every seat full. An old man rises at the other end.
" O, don't rise," said the lovely girl. "I don't care whether you sit or stand," he replied, "I'm going to get out,"

———:o:———

The receipts for the last night of Mr. and Mrs. W. J. Florence, at the Grand Opera House, New York, amounted to $3,864, the largest amount of money ever received for one performance at the Grand Opera House.

———:o:———

Two little girls were lately prattling together, and one of them said : " We keep four servants, have got six horses, and lots of carriages. Now what have you got ?" With quite as much pride the other answered :—" We've dot a skunk under our barn."

standing room occupied." While large in numbers, the audience lacked something in manners:

. . . We have nothing to say by way of advice to the noisy crowd of ragamuffins whose demoniac yells and screeches, accompanied by the beating of their hoofs, shocked ears polite last evening. They are simply a nuisance . . . There is another class of disturbers not peculiar to Wilmington who invariably commence the bustle of departure five minutes before the close of any performance . . .[3]

Wilmington audiences gave the company an excellent reception, but obviously Wilmington audiences were not considered sophisticated and they were short changed during a performance of *Oliver Twist*. At the end of the fourth act

Wallack appeared before the curtain and thanked the audience for the courtesy he had received in our city and said the play is ended. The audience of course left, but the fact is that the play had not been finished as there is another act . . . the truth is the actors wanted to get away that night and were guilty of a somewhat shabby trick.[4]

Opening the Opera House with a series of dramatic performances was significant in that dramatic performances including comedies, tragedies, melodramas, spectacles and the later appendages, *i.e.*, vaudeville and burlesque, were always the dominant form of entertainment at the Opera House.

A few days after the Wallack-Richings troupe departed, another form of entertainment was introduced—the lecture. Reverend Dr. Henson delivered a "witty, wise, brilliant talk" on "Money or the Golden Calf." In February, a Mr. Hutching presented two illustrated lectures on California and the Yo Semite Valley. At the end of the month, one of the nation's outstanding lecturers, Daniel Dougherty, delivered a talk entitled "The Stage," a defense of the stage which was still considered a "damnable sin" by many Wilmington church leaders and God fearing men. While emphasizing the value of the stage, Mr. Dougherty argued that the stage could be its own worst enemy:

By pandering to depraved taste, by the introduction of the licentious ballet and the flimsy spectacular drama, where only gaudy lascivious objects are presented and where the eye and not the mind is called upon to judge . . .[5]

Mr. Dougherty urged all citizens to drive such wretched representations away by patronizing nothing but what was good and calculated to exercise a beneficial effect.

On January 8, the first minstrel troupe arrived at the Opera House and attracted a large and enthusiastic audience. Minstrel shows—performances of singing, dancing and gagging by white men with blackened faces, later by true blacks—became an enormously popular form of entertainment during the last half of the 19th century. Although there were only two minstrel performances during the first season (one by Robert Fraser's Minstrel and Pantomime Troupe and one by Simmons and Slocum's Minstrels) in later years there were often as many as ten to twelve.

Wilmington audiences were most enthusiastic about the parade of national stars and troupes which the new Opera House hosted. When the brilliant and popular Maggie Mitchell made her debut in *Fanchon the Cricket* and *Jane Eyre* in late January, the audience was totally entranced:

Maggie Mitchell had a most successful debut—were it not for the foolish green cards stuck up about the theatre forbidding "excessive demonstration of applause," she would have brought the house down.[6]

Before the February arrival of Fanny Janauschek, the "queen of tragedy," Wilmington critics felt it necessary to alert the public to her importance:

We say unhesitatingly that such an opportunity was never before presented to a Wilmington audience, and we hope our people will demonstrate that Wilmington can respond properly to such.[7]

Indeed, the response to Janauschek's performance of *Maria Stuart* was gratifying:

Every seat was filled and standing room was partially occupied. A more cultivated and intelligent audience was never drawn together in our city.[8]

M. Janauschek's diamonds and jewels were equally popular. Crowds of people flocked to Thomas Boughman and Co., the local bookstore, where Mrs. Janauschek's jewelry collection valued at more than $100,000 was on display—proving once again that diamonds are a girl's best friend.

On March 12 Mr. E. L. Davenport, one of the nation's outstanding tragedians, gave the first of his numerous Wilmington appearances in *A New Way To Pay Old Debts*. His presentation was labeled "powerful and lifelike."

Maggie Mitchell

Fanny Janauschek

Later in March, the Florence Stock Co., a well-known comedy troupe performed for three nights. The company was "greeted with applause each evening and kept listeners in continual uproar."

Not all of the popular stars of the day were supported in Wilmington. Junius Brutus Booth, who was acclaimed as the nation's leading Shakespearian actor, played to exceedingly small audiences. His appearances, which were financial disasters, indicated Wilmington's continual lack of support for Shakespearian drama.

The new Opera House provided numerous novel entertainment experiences in February. A military fair, open day and night during the first six days of the month, included loading, firing, and formation drills as well as a musical concert. Major General George G. Meade, hero of Gettysburg, was the major attraction. During future seasons, the Opera House was often set up for a fair or dime show which attracted droves of people all day and night.

On February 15 a Children's Jubilee was held. One thousand children dressed in white sang to benefit the Grand Army of the Republic. The performance was well attended and praised immensely. Local groups continually used the Opera House and were well supported. More often than not, a local performance received an overflowing audience and enthusiastic encouragement.

The Washington Fire Company held its first annual ball in the Opera House on February 22. Given the enormous success of the ball, the company continued to use the Opera House for many years. Numerous social functions were held annually in the theatre which could be transformed into a ballroom by fitting a wooden floor over the stage and parquet area.

Despite the fact that the theatre was called an Opera House, Opera played a relatively minor rôle. During the initial season there was only one full scale opera, *Martha,* by the Parepa Rosa Grand English Opera Company. Labelled the musical event of the season, *Martha* was attended by a large audience. One operatic concert was held in May.

The initial season at the Opera House would not have been complete without a performance of *Uncle Tom's Cabin,* the play based on Harriet Beecher Stowe's novel. The most popular American play of the 19th century, it was performed twice in April. Before the first performance, the *Every Evening* reported: *Uncle Tom's Cabin* has been received with enthusiasm for years, but it has never been presented in this city so it is presumable many of our people have not seen it" . . .[9]

PERFORMANCE INDEX*

* This is part of a complete performance index from 1872-1910
which, hopefully, will be published at some future date.

Concerts played a small role in the Opera House. Of the four concerts given during 1871-1872, none were well attended. After the Theodore Thomas concert in April the papers complained: "the small size of the audience reflects little credit on the people of the town."

When the Rossini Quintette and Sixtette played in February, barely one hundred people attended. The *Every Evening* critic commented: "if ever first class artists played to a beggarly array of empty benches, they did last evening at the Opera House."[10]

By the time the Opera House closed for the summer of 1872, it had hosted more than 70 performances. Never had the cultural life in Wilmington been so active.

Opposition Line !   Prices Reduced !

Franklin Telegraph Co.

Lines East, West, North & South.

TERMS AND CONDITIONS.

The rules of this Company require that all messages received for transmission shall be written on the message blanks of the Company, under and subject to the conditions printed thereon.

J. W. BROWN, Pres.   J. G. SMITH, Supt.

BLANK No. 1.

Feb 12th 1872

By Telegraph from Baltimore Md

To J. P. Allmond

Masonic Temple

Please give me the refusal of Tuesday and Wednesday twenty first and second

H. C. Ford

Please answer

DH

This message has just been received at the office.

Nr 2 W Brook St

MUDGE & SON, PRINTERS AND STATIONERS, BOSTON.

The Masonic Hall Company, which managed the theatre, received numerous telegrams requesting use of the hall

In order to maintain strict control over the theatre, the Masonic Hall Co. chose to handle all rental arrangements through its own Board of Directors. One of the Company's first tasks was to outline a rental fee schedule. In October 1871 the Masons established the original fee schedule: $300 for balls, $100 for theatrical events, $60 for lectures, $75 for concerts, and $50 for Sunday school concerts. Although the schedule did govern the first season, it was continually adjusted downward during the next five years.

During the last third of the nineteenth century the combination system grew to dominate the economic organization of theatre. Under the combination system, a temporary company was formed to produce one play which toured the entire country.[11] The unity between producing plays and managing theatres was gone; local managers became real estate operators. Built at an opportune time, and in a central location between Philadelphia and Baltimore, the Grand Opera House attracted the immediate attention of performers and agents and became an important booking house.

In 1871, the pre-telephone days, all requests for the theatre were telegrams and letters sent by stars, agents, and theatre managers. Telegrams which conveyed their message succinctly were sent a few days prior to the desired performance date. Actor Horace Lingard sent the following telegram ten days before an anticipated performance: "Book me 2 nights commencing February 22—answer immediately." In February, Ford telegramed from Baltimore: "Give me refusal of Tuseday and Wednesday, February 21 and 22." Letters

usually requested additional information. In December, Tony Pastor wrote: "Book the Tony Pastor Troupe from Wednesday, May 22.

I will send $50 on Monday. Is the hall a new one? What are the payment terms?" E. K. Kendall, Manager of the Abbott Pantomime Troupe, wrote to request Monday, Tuesday, and Wednesday, April 1, 2, and 3. He added: "Write me at the Holliday Street Theatre in Baltimore and state the rent and capacity of the house and what you will furnish."

By carefully reviewing all applications for the hall and screening out the undesirable ones, the Masons established some basic management policies. Permission to give a temperance lecture was denied to Reverend R. B. McDonald in December. A firm stand against political meetings was taken with the following resolution passed at the January 5, 1872 meeting:

Whereas in cities of the size of Wilmington during political campaigns many political meetings are held and such generally seek the most commodious hall for these purposes and in as much as this class of assemblages are composed of people who have little care of the furniture of the hall and greatly injure and damage the same, Be it resolved that the Building Committee be instructed to refuse our hall for all political meetings and to all assemblages whose managers do not charge a fee of admission.

(Both of these policies were reversed by 1876, and the Opera House became an important meeting center for political and temperance groups.) Later in the month, when the committee learned that Mr. Ford was planning to bring Lidia Thompson, the forerunner of burlesque, to the Opera House, it immediately informed him that she would not be permitted to perform.

Despite the strict management policies of the Masonic Hall Co., the Opera House fell prey to severe church criticism. The opposition preached from the pulpits and stated its case strongly in the newspapers. In February Reverend James H. Lightbourn denounced theatre by saying "the only way to justify the stage is to condemn the Bible." His letter to the *Delaware Republican* stated:

Permit me in conclusion to suggest that those who have control of the Masonic Temple disabuse the public mind that the theatre is under the auspices of Freemasonry. . . . There is no cable tow long enough or strong enough to draw me to a theatre or Opera House.
. . . If a young man acquires a taste for this species of entertainment, he is in danger of becoming a lost character. All the evils that can waste his property, corrupt his morals, blast his reputation, embitter life and destroy the soul lurk in the purliens of a theatre.[12]

59

Ford's Opera House, Baltimore

The advocates, like Daniel Dougherty, defended the stage just as strongly.

Throughout the inaugural season two agents, Mr. Ford and the Citizens Entertainment Association, sponsored a large percentage of the performances. As the manager of two Baltimore theatres, Mr. Ford controlled some of the country's top entertainments and provided Wilmington with outstanding events. During the 1871-1872 season, he was responsible for bringing Maggie Mitchell, Jane Coombs, Junius Brutus Booth, comedian Robert Owens, the famous Hernandez Foster Pantomime Co., and the Humpty Dumpty Co. as well as the first performance of *Uncle Tom's Cabin*.

Performances given under Mr. Ford's auspices were so successful that shortly after the opening, the *Delaware Republican* stated:

Mr. Ford is fortunate in securing the best talent of the country and in producing none but the most chaste and popular plays for our citizens and has won himself a high degree of popular favor.[13]

Apparently Mr. Ford was not equally content. Several of his events did not attract the audiences he had anticipated. After the particularly unsuccessful attendance at the performances of Booth, Mr.

Ford complained bitterly that he had lost an average of $200 every night of Mr. Booth's stay. Mr. Ford disagreed with the policy of charging more by the week. More cautious in future seasons, Mr. Ford limited the number of events he sponsored at the Opera House. He never again tried to bring a full schedule of performances to the Grand theatre. However, Mr. Ford's initial interest did establish an important pattern—Wilmington was now part of a traveling circuit; outstanding touring events always stopped at the Wilmington Grand.

The Citizen's Entertainment Association was a group of local gentlemen who organized in February, 1872 in order "to secure first class entertainment for the new Opera House." The committee, which was on the list of managers of dramatic agencies in New York and Philadelphia, was responsible for the performances by Madame Janauschek in February. In March, the Citizen's Entertainment Committee sponsored the return of Jane Coombs who had played successfully under the management of Mr. Ford. When the Citizen's Entertainment Committee requested permission to lease the hall for the entire 1872-1873 season it was refused by the Masonic Hall Co. who stated that it wanted control of the house for at least the present year. One year later, by the end of the spring of 1873, relations with the Citizen's Entertainment Committee and it leader Frank Nolan had deteriorated despite the success of the events sponsored by the committee. The committee and the Masonic Hall Co. argued about Mr. Nolan's practice of advertising himself as manager of the Opera House and about his practice of reserving dates and later cancelling them at the last minute. The Masonic Hall Co. seemed to resent the Committee's interference. By 1874, the Citizen's Entertainment Committee had dropped from the Opera House picture.

By the close of the first season, the Masons could be proud. Not only had they provided Wilmington with high caliber entertainment, but they had brought in about $8,207. Pleased with their endeavor, the Masons continued to manage the theatre themselves until 1888.

OPERA HOUSE PROGRAMME
WILMINGTON DELAWARE.

VOL. IV. No. 24   WEDNESDAY EVENING, NOVEMBER 15th, 1882.

J. F. SPECK, PUBLISHER AND PRINTER.

The Premium
FIRE-PLACE HEATER.

There is a large variety of FIRE-PLACE HEATERS on the market, many of them having good qualities, all of which are contained in the "Premium," in addition to which it has several new and important *improvements*, which are as follows:

1st. A Dome which is entirely new in its construction in this Heater, in which a separate chamber is formed, in which the hot gases are collected before passing to the smoke pipe. It is controlled by a damper, which damper is also used to give direct draft when kindling the fire.

2d. A peculiarly constructed back radiator, which forms a part of the combustion chamber. It is cone-shaped, with a series of pipes starting at the bottom of combustion chamber and leading to the dome pipes and radiator, all cast in one solid piece and very heavy, so that there is no chance for the escape of gas into the hot air chamber. By this construction of dome and back radiator, the products of combustion are caused to reverberate and are thrown back into the combustion chamber, filling the same with highly heated gases, which with the flame impinging the radiator pipes, and the mica front, makes it the most powerful Heater for the room in which it stands as well as for the rooms above.

3d. The Fire Pot is suspended, leaving a large hot air space between it and the outer casing of the Heater, so that the air which supports combustion is highly heated before entering the fire pot, thus producing a hot air draft, the result of which is perfect combustion of and perfect consumption of gases.

This fire pot is made in sections, as is also the magazine, so that either can be repaired or new ones put in without removing the heater from the fire-place in which it sets. It is very simple and not liable to get out of order.

4th. The Grate vibrates, and is made with one-half slide to make convenient opening for dumping or to remove clinkers.

5th. There is no flue in the base of this heater, so that ample space is afforded for a large ash-pan, and the annoyance of cleaning flue avoided. In these points all other heaters are deficient.

SCHOEN'S
HEATER, RANGE AND STOVE HOUSE,
No. 209 to 213 Shipley St., Wilmington, Del.

The Favorite Heater.

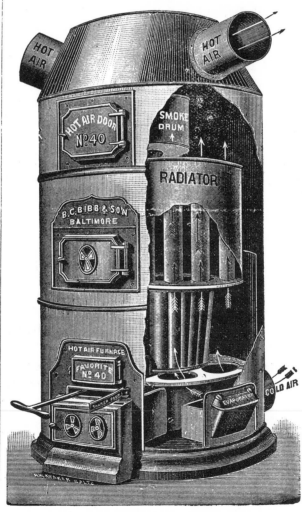

THE MOST ECONOMICAL, DURABLE, AND
GIVES PERFECT SATISFACTION.
Call and see it at
JAMES F. WOOD & CO.,
FRONT & ORANGE STREETS.

'What made the mule kick you?" they asked of the gentleman who had been sent through the roof of a barn. And he answered: "Do you think I was fool enough to go back and ask him?

Gracie's first experience in eating a peach: "I've eaten it, cloth and all, mamma; now what shall I do with the bone?"

To think properly one must think independently, candidly, and consecutively; only in this way can a train of reasoning be conducted successfully.

RENDERING good for good, he is the most generous who begins; rendering evil for evil, he is most unjust who begins.

OUR good deeds rarely cause smuch gossip among our neighbors, but our evil ones leap immediately into notoriety.

SCENE TWO

ESTABLISHMENT OF AN ENTERTAINMENT MAGNET

1872-1888

The Opera House was the undisputed center of entertainment in Wilmington from 1871-1886. Althought events were held at the Wilmington Institute, the Odd Fellows Building, the Wilmington Roller Rink, and a variety of churches, none hosted the same number or caliber of events as the Opera House. Not until the Academy of Music opened in January 1886 did the Opera House have any significant competitor, but even then both houses drew large crowds. As one critic stated in May 1886: "there has been a better line of attractions than there has been in three or four years."

During the sixteen years of home management, when the Opera House was managed by the Masonic Hall Co., even the worst years brought at least 65 performances to the Opera House; good years provided closer to 140 performances. The enthusiasm of the initial season was sustained over the next two seasons, each of which provided more than 100 performances. Beginning in 1874-1875 the Opera House declined, reaching its nadir during the 1876-1877 season when only 65 performances were held. A business depression was widely acclaimed as the reason for the decline. After the disasterous 1876-1877 season the performance level increased quickly, so that by the early 1880s performances again numbered well over 100. While competing with the Academy of Music, the Opera House hosted more than 130 performances in 1885-1886 and 1886-1887, and nearly 120 performances in 1887-1888—thereby demonstrating that Wilmington could support two theatres.

Obviously the nature of the performances varied greatly during the years; however, the dominance of national events was maintained. Local groups like the Tuesday Club, Millard Club, Philharmonic Club, and Choral Club did perform at the theatre and were enthusiastically supported by huge audiences, which were often bigger than those greeting professional outsiders. But the largest number of performances was given by professional groups who toured the entire country.

63

Dramatic Events

Dramatic performances, always the largest single category of events, account for nearly one-half of all performances in most seasons.

During the 1870s comedies were very popular. When John T. Raymond appeared in Mark Twain's *Gilded Age* in 1875 the audience of some 900 people was "convulsed with laughter."

The Boucicault Comedy Company presented *Forbidden Fruit* in February, 1887 and attracted one of the largest audiences ever at the Opera House.

One of the greatest events of the season was Barney Williams, one of the nation's best comedians, playing in *Fairy Circle*. After one of the immensely popular comedies of the Florence Company, a local critic explained the popularity of comedy: "It's the kind of performance that hundreds prefer, a good laugh after a day's work does more than a long night's sleep." [1]

Western dramas, which capitalized on public interest in Western expansion, were also popular during the 1870s. When Buffalo Bill, the well known hunter, actor and legislator, opened on December 3 and 4, 1874 in *Scout of the Plains* he attracted a large audience and was praised for his superior acting. During another of his numerous appearances he appeared in *The Red Right Hand* on October 21, 1878, and the audience filled the house: "the largest of the season . . . the gallery was packed and standing room only downstairs." [2] In March 1874 Frank Mayo presented *Davy Crockett* to a reasonably large audience and set the gallery "wild with delights." The local critic was less enthusiastic. He suggested the play should be rewritten to fill the public's love for adventure without violating all probability. In 1883 Mayo took his large audience by storm. Almost every sentence was greeted with laughter or applause.

Comedies and border dramas were a continual source of delight, but by the 1880s spectacles and melodramas began to appear with great frequency. Spectacles, plays with elaborate scenic effects, were produced most often during the 1882-1883 season. In January 1883 *The Devil's Auction,* a pantomime in three acts, featured pantomimists, ballet troups, and skating acts. Billed as the grandest spectacle of an age, the play drew an enormous audience. While praised for its brilliant scenic effects, the play was criticized for shockingly bad music by a local orchestra.

In October 1883 the spectacular drama, *The World,* premièred before the largest audience of the season. Some called the play a spectacular drama superbly mounted; others labelled it a hackneyed melodrama with features of scenic beauty. In either case, large, demonstrative audiences continued to attend performances of *The World* for numerous years.

Melodramas rose to extreme popularity during the early 1880s, much to the critics' disapproval. After a performance of *Young Mrs. Winthrop* in 1883 the *Every Evening* critic bemoaned the popularity of melodrama: "the play was very good for its kind, but we feel the whole class of highly wrought melo-dramas richly deserves to perish

65

from the stage." [3] *The Silver King* was an enormously popular melodrama which appealed to the audience by running the whole scale of emotions from pathetic to tragic, with a sprinkling of comedy. After the first performance of the play, local critics commented: "Wilmington play patrons again gave a practical expression of their preferences for plays of melodramatic school, in the large audience which assembled to see *The Silver King.*" [4] In 1885, the melodrama trend slackened slightly. After a performance of *Burr Oaks,* the local critic stated: "as far as the season has gone, attendance indicates that the sensational drama is losing its popularity, yet Wilmington has lots of it." [5]

In contrast, serious drama did not fare well. The critics' perpetual lament was that the audience was smaller than the merits of the performance deserved. As early as October 1872, when the public failed to support a performance of *Rose of Castille,* by the Richings-Bernard troupe, the trend against serious drama became evident: "There is a deepening impression that our people are unwilling to support a really first rate entertainment. This company is really a good one and if people fail to support it, they will have to put up with poor ones or none." [6]

In 1878 when the Warde and Barrymore Dramatic Company, one of the better dramatic companies ever to give a representation in Wilmington, performed *Diplomacy,* only 300-400 people attended. Unfortunately the trend didn't change much. Ten years later, when *Held by the Enemy* (the best dramatic event of the season), was hailed as an artistic success, it only attracted a very small audience.

The local reception of Shakespeare was disasterous. During the initial season, Booth had failed to draw a proper audience. Whenever Shakespeare was attempted, the lament of small audiences was repeated: in 1872, *Hamlet,* Edwin Booth; in 1876, *Julius Caesar.* When the popular Frank Mayo of *Davy Crockett* fame appeared in *Hamlet* in 1882, even he failed to attract an audience of any size. An irrate critic stated sarcastically: ". . . blood hounds and blood and thunder tableau present attractions to Wilmingtonians which the bard of Avon seems unable to offer." [7]

Right: William F. Cody—"Buffalo Bill"

Wilmington audiences were decidedly steadfast in their tastes. Popular stars like Maggie Mitchell, Charlotte Thompson, Annie Pixley, Joe Jefferson, John T. Raymond, and E. L. Davenport were well supported on their numerous Opera House visits. Charlotte Thompson appeared at least 12 times between 1873 and 1886; she was the Christmas attraction in 1876, 1877, 1878, 1880 and 1882. Maggie Mitchell, who often repeated the same dramas, especially *Fanchon the Cricket*, was a great Wilmington favorite. In 1885, Miss Mitchell was praised for her enduring talent: "she is simply the same as she has been for a quarter of a century, incomparable in the comedy roles she interprets." [8]

W. J. Florence and Joseph Jefferson

When the great comedian, Joseph Jefferson, starred in *Rip Van Winkle* on May 18, 1888, the house was packed:

composed in main of older play goers, including very many whose faces are rarely seen in public places of amusement. The opportunity to see the great artist at his best was sufficient pretext for many to lay aside their prejudice . . .[9]

MATINEES

Wednesday and Saturday.

ANNIE PIXLEY

In her great Impersonation

M'LISS

John T. Raymond, another famed comedian, performed in Wilmington innumerable times. After his performance of *For Congress* in 1884, the *Every Evening* reported: "seldom is a Wilmington audience, proverbially cold, roused to such enthusiasm." [10]

Lillian Langtry is another of the "greats" who, like Booth, never quite made it in Wilmington. After her performances in May 1883 in *Pygmalion* and *Galatea,* a local critic had these unflattering words:

Is Mrs. Langtry beautiful? . . . it may be safely affirmed that of the 1200 people who saw her—not one will deny her a handsome figure, a majestic presence and a graceful manner. At the same time, however, few could fail to see her mouth is wide, her nose far from perfect, while even the least experienced theatre goer must have recognized the practical justness of the general critical verdict that she is at best an amateur actress of very moderate skill. [11]

Her performance of *Mademoiselle Mars* in March 1903 failed to attract a large audience, but the local critic attributed the small attendance to the abominable weather and the top notch price of $2.00.

Sarah Bernhardt is the great star who did *not* appear at the Grand, but because she almost did, her "appearance" has become legendary. The highlight of the 1880-1881 season would have been the appearance of Sarah Bernhardt in *Camille* on December 28. In the middle of December, the *Every Evening* assured the public "The Bernhardt *is* coming" and will be supported by the same company of French artists that played in New York and Boston. Just one week later, the *Every Evening* was forced to report "Bernhardt Backs Down." The event was cancelled because of the unfavorable prospects for such financial support as would warrant "the divine Sarah in giving us a visit." In order to pay for the event the manager needed a full house, but only about $250 worth of tickets had been sold. Mademoiselle Bernhardt was to receive $500 exclusive of expenses which included a special train from Springfield. The critic advised people to go elsewhere where the prospects of support were better.

One of the most popular theatre troupes in Wilmington was the Madison Square Company, one of the foremost companies in the nation managed by the Frohman Brothers and directed by David Belasco. It appeared at least eleven times between 1881 and 1890 in

*One of the numerous Uncle Tom's Cabin Companies that visited
Wilmington, in front of the Wilmington firm that made this
particular railroad car*

such popular plays as *Young Mrs. Winthrop* and *Jim the Penman.*
Usually theatre goers came out in full force and filled the theatre
beyond seating capacity.

Uncle Tom's Cabin, which had been performed twice in the
opening season, continued to be a great favorite. The play was repeated no less than 21 times between 1872 and 1888. As early as 1878,
one critic suggested that the small house could be explained by the
frequent repetition of the play. In spite of the repetition there were
always several hundred people in the audience. The size of the audience varied according to the troupe. During the 1881-1882 season
alone, the play was presented four times. But by the 1880s the critics,
tired of the play, rarely took the time to review it.

The trend of patronizing the best known stars, troupes, and
plays was explained by an editorial in the *Evening Programme*
which defended the tastes of Wilmington theatre goers:

Now it must be admitted that Wilmington is decidedly conservative in
many ways, and in none more so than in the matter of dealing with strangers. . . . There is probably no city where people who have been long
established and are well and favorably known have a more decided advantage over recent comers; and this applies to business of all sorts, theatrical
as well as others.[12]

Opera

Although the new Masonic theatre was called a Grand Opera House, relatively few performances of opera were held each season. During the 1870s the number of operas, often *opéra bouffe*, per season varied between one and eight performances and were attended by only a small, select audience. In 1874 a performance by the Kellogg Troupe, which had played to capacity crowds at Ford's Theatre in Baltimore, was cancelled because too few tickets were sold after some Wilmingtonians "insisted on arraigning and condemning the troupe unheard." In 1873 Wilmington lost a very fine musical entertainment, the Hyer Sisters and their colored Operatic troupe, by failure to support. According to reports: "after waiting until some time after 8 for an audience, the number of persons in the hall not exceeding 50, most in the gallery, it was announced not enough people were present for a performance."[13] Based on its rendition of one quartet, the troupe was praised for its rare ability.

But during the early 1880s opera became increasingly popular; 17 performances were given in the 1882-1883 season. Three seasons between 1884 and 1887 were the heyday of opera. Since several troupes remained in residency for a full week, the performance level increased to over 25 per season. The Bennett and Moulton Comic Opera Co., which specialized in comic and light operas, was in residency for one week during the 1884-1885 season. In the review of *Chimes of Normandy* the *Every Evening* stated: "over 2,200 people attended; not for a long time has the auditorium been so solidly packed with humanity."[14]

When the Boston Ideal Opera Company gave three performances in February of the same season, large enthusiastic audiences attended because opera had become fashionable:

many of the ladies were in full evening dress and there was a profusion of flowers and rich effects in colors which made a pleasing scene. Boxes were occupied by private theatre parties, who have initiated a custom here which has long been in vogue in other cities.[15]

The Harris Opera Company, one of Wilmington's favorite operatic troupes, played for one week in May 1885, and then returned for several performances in the fall. Their performance of *La Mascotte* in September 1885 attracted 1,957 people, including

❊The ✢ Programme.❊

Published and Printed by the Mercantile Printing Company, No. 714 Market Street.

The Programme is the only authorized house bill of the Opera House, and is published by the Mercantile Printing Company, under agreement with, and by exclusive authority of the Board of Directors, of the Masonic Hall Company.

Advertisers desiring changes of matter or new advertisements inserted, must send copy to our office before twelve o'clock noon, on day of performance.

WEDNESDAY MATINEE, OCT. 28, 1885.

The man about town of the *Star* takes occasion to criticise the quality and quantity of the Programme. We do not propose to make an entire new paper every day, but to change the reading matter as frequently as we deem necessary or convenient. It is not to be presumed that the Opera House is frequented by the same people every night, and therefore we conclude that an entire change of matter is not necessary to keep the paper from growing stale. We are not unwilling to have a comparison in any respect made between our paper, and that of any of our predecessors. In regard to the limitation as to quantity, there is no limit put upon us except the capacity of the house. Whenever the occasion requires it, we shall print Programmes for every seat in the house, above and below, above that number we feel under no special obligations to go.

The revival of business which we suggested in a previous article some weeks ago, seems about to be realized. There are so many signs of returning prosperity, that the people are growing perceptably buoyant with hope. They are emerging from their long season of depression, and soon the streets will be deserted by the men who have been so long walking about in enforced idleness. The work shops will call them away.

The Wilmington and Citizen's polo team will play a match game to-morrow, Wednesday evening, at the Wilmington Rink. The game will be exciting and interesting, and will doubtless well attended, as it should.

Programme for the Matinee.

BENNETT & MOULTEN'S

COMIC OPERA CO.

An entirely new and original Japanese Comic Opera, in Two Acts, entitled.

➤➣➤⊙ T H E ⊙⊷⊰⊷

MIKADO !

Or, the Town of TITIPU.

❊CAST ✦ OF ✦ CHARACTERS.❊

The Mikado of Japan . . . . Frank B. Molten

Nanki-Poo . . . . Carl Alberte
His son, disguised as a wandering minstrel, and in love with Yum-Yum.

Ko-Ko, lord high executioner of Titipu . . . . . . E. P. Smith

Pooh-Bah, lord high everything else . . . . Ben Lodge

Pish-Tush, a noble lord . . . . Arthur E. Miller

Yum-Yum, ⎫
Pitti-Sing, ⎬ sisters, wards of Ko-Ko ⎬
Peep-Bo, ⎭
Miss Bessie Fairbairn
. . Miss Irine Murphy
. Miss Carie Sweeney

Katisha, an elderly lady in love with Nanki-Poo
Miss Annie Carter

Nee-Ban . . . . P. M. Lang
Chorus of School-girls, nobles, guards and coolies.

Moulton & Baker, ... Proprietors and Managers
M. C. Smith, ... Musical Director
E. P. Smith, ... Stage Manager
P. M. Lang, ... Assistant Stage Manager

[SEE THIRD PAGE FOR SYNOPSIS.]

the most discriminating play goers and musicians. The company was so delighted with its hearty reception that it promised to return a few months later.

When the National Opera Company performed *Lakme* in 1887, about 1,600 people, the leading social element of the city, were present. The elaborate performance illustrated that the composition of musical masters could be interpreted on the Opera House stage with the same detail and artistic effect as in large cities. During these years the same operas, including *La Mascotte, Chimes of Normandy, Patience,* and *Mikado* were repeated *ad nauseum* but they continued to draw crowds. However, the intense heyday of opera was short lived. When Proctor and Soulier assumed managament of the theatre in 1888, the frequency of operatic events again declined.

Concerts

During most seasons, not more than seven concerts were given, and concerts by nationally recognized stars were often poorly attended. After nearly every concert, the familiar lament that the audience was smaller than the merits of the performance deserved was repeated. After the concert of violin virtuoso Camilla Urso in 1885 the *Every Evening* reported:

it is humiliating to repeat on the reoccurrance of each noteworthy musical event, deserving of patronage, that the small audiences are not only discouraging to the artists but a discredit to a city of Wilmington's size and pretensions.[16]

When the Mendelssohn Quintette Club performed, an irate critic chided:

Any musical Wilmingtonian away from home would be ashamed to say that in his city of over 50,000 people hardly 200 went to hear a concert by such a celebrated musical organization as the Mendelssohn Club and yet such is the fact.[17]

Despite its small size, the audience was usually appreciative and enthusiastic. A few concerts, particularly the orchestra and band concerts, did attract very large audiences.

In contrast, musical events by local groups were generally supported. Concerts by The Old Folks, the Tuesday Club, Millard Club, and the Philharmonic Society became annual events attracting large, enthusiastic audiences.

CAMILLA URSO'S CONCERT.

CAMILLA URSO,

ASSISTED BY

MISS IVY WANDESFORDE, Soprano.   MR. W. C. TOWER, Tenor.

MR. J. F. RUDOLPHSEN, Baritone.   HERR BENNO SCHEREK, Solo-Pianist.

FREDERIC LUER, Director.

PROVIDENT SOCIETY COURSE,

WILMINGTON, DEL.,

GRAND OPERA HOUSE,

Oct. 27. CAMILLA URSO CONCERT.

Nov. 15.—STUART ROGERS. PERSONATIONS.
Dec. 11.—MENDELSSOHN QUARTETTE CLUB.
Dec. 20.—HON. N. P. BANKS. LECTURE.
Jan. 8.—EMMA ABBOTT CONCERT.

Tickets for Sale by Lady Managers and C. J. Thomas & Co.

Lew Dockstader and the Primrose and West Minstrels

Minstrel Shows

Many of the major companies, including Primrose and West, Lew Dockstader, Carncross & Dixey, and Callender's Georgia played at the Opera House almost every season. During most seasons there were as many as twelve minstrel performances with the same troupes often appearing several times in one season. Carncross Minstrels appeared at least thirteen times between 1873 and 1883. In May 1879, 2,200 people attended a performance which netted a larger profit than any which had been gathered at the Masonic Temple since it was built. Barlow, Wilson, Primrose, and West—acclaimed nationally as one of the finest minstrel troupes—gave eight performances in just three seasons during the early 1880s. Minstrel groups often opened the season in August and closed it in May or June. Local critics, who rarely took the time to discuss the minstrel shows, constantly bemoaned the great public patronage afforded to mistrel shows and denied to performances of more merit.

Variety Shows

Despite Daniel Dougherty's warnings against patronizing the licentious ballet and the spectacular drama, variety shows and burlesque did play at the Opera House.

Vaudeville, a form of variety show, which in its early days was considered too vulgar for ladies, was made into clean, family entertainment during the 1860s and 1870s largely through the efforts of Tony Pastor who had visited the Opera House numerous times beginning with the opening season. In 1875, he presented a program featuring gymnasts, duelists, musicians, and comedians. On April 20, 1878 the Tony Pastor troupe performed a variety program which included farces, ventriloquial feats, imitations, and a musical mélange using ox horns and gas pipes. The performance delighted the audience, and the *Every Evening* critic commented: "seldom indeed is our city visited by a variety troupe capable of giving such an entertainment." [18]

Numerous variety troupes, often called museums in order to give themselves an air of legitimacy, appeared at the Opera House. In January 1884 H. R. Jacobs's Royal Museum and Novelty Co. featured "Hop O My Thumb," a human mite who was only 21 inches high. The show, which only charged 10 cents admission, featured ventriloquists, roller skaters, and midgets. Admiral Dot's London Museum presented a magical delusionist as well as a ventriloquist.

Burlesque

Burlesque began as a travesty of a serious play or event. When leg art was added in the 1860s the nature of the performances changed dramatically. In 1871 the Masonic Hall Company forbade the appearance of Lydia Thompson, the forerunner of burlesque, even though she was drawing large crowds in other cities. However, *Black Crook,* an extravaganza which gained national acclaim despite the complaint that it was merely gorgeous scenes and gams. appeared at the Opera House innumerable times. The Rentz-Santley Novelty & Burlesque Company performed annually during the 1880s. The company's performance of *Pinafore* in March 1880 attracted an "audience of 1,000, only half a dozen of whom were women." The *Every Evening* called the audience "the nearest approach to a unanimously male audience ever seen here at a theatrical entertainment." In September, 1884, the Rentz-Santley Company presented an exhibition of "homely women in paint, powder and the most provocative costumes" to an audience of 500 men and boys. Although burlesque was performed, it never reached large proportions at the Opera House.

Every season a variety of unclassifiable performances were held. One of the most popular attractions was Bartholew's Equine Paradox. Marvelous horse tricks were performed for a solid week and drew large crowds. Theatre also incorporated the newest intellectual ideas and scientific developments. In September 1877 a concert was given by Edison's electromotograph, popularly referred to as the "singing telephone" in order to distinguish it from the talking telephone. The device transmitted music from the Western Union Telegraph Office in Philadelphia to the stage of the Opera House where it was installed. A lecture explaining the technological aspects of the machine accompanied the concert. Despite the importance of the concert, Wilmingtonians failed to show up thereby enraging the critics:

The people of this city don't deserve an Opera House. or any hall where a performance that is worth seeing or hearing can be given.
. . . A second rate minstrel show or some low variety performance can always be certain of a full house in Wilmington, but let a really meritorious entertainment favor the city with a visit and it is equally sure of being greeted by empty benches. In this respect the instincts of Wilmingtonians are unerring and they are very rarely fooled into patronizing a good performance.[19]

In June 1878 there were three exhibitions daily of Edison's phonograph, which was labelled the ninth wonder of the age. Advertisements boasted: "It laughs, it sings, it talks, it whistles, and it plays coronet solos."

In these pre-moving picture days, Professor Cromwell's Art Entertainments were another unique event. The professor used pictures twenty feet high to accompany his talks on London, Paris, and the Swiss Alps. The views were proclaimed "works of art in themselves," which gave the public the opportunity of seeing places in foreign lands. The talks were dubbed "genuine banquets in an intellectual sense."

An interest in magic was rampant. Hermann the Predigitateur, Dr. Wiljalba Frikell, and Dr. Gomez were among the magicians who dazzled the public with unusual tricks. While magic was acceptable, spiritualism was strictly forbidden. In December 1875 an exhibition of spiritualism in which tables would float in the air and spirits walk on the stage was advertised. Mayor Whitely wrote a letter forbidding such a repugnant exhibition, but President Lobdell had already cancelled the performance, which had been mistakenly booked. Mr. Lobdell stated that his influence was always used in favor of religion and morality: "While I am President, the hall will never be used for improper performances." Through exposure to the national trends, attitudes changed quickly. In January 1877 a magic show entitled "Spirit Power in the Light" by two renowned materialistic mediums did take place before a large audience. And by 1882 when Annie Eva Fay, the spiritualist, performed, she drew a large, mixed audience: "several prominent citizens, minds of scientific and philosophical channels and a gentle sprinkling of long haired dreamy eyed individuals." [20] In 1884 Lulu Hurst, the Georgian wonder, completely mystified the spectators with manifestations of supernatural power like making a chair fly.

Numerous balls were held in the theatre. The Washington Fire Co. held their annual ball here for many years. Elaborate decorations added to the festivity of the 1875 ball: "the balcony posts, front and proscenium boxes were arrayed with evergreens, looped and trimmed; the stage was arranged to represent a garden." [21]

In the late 1870s Professor Webster, who later ran a dancing academy on the upper floors, began renting the theatre for grand parties. On Christmas Day 1878 a dancing matinée was presented by his students. On February 19, 1878 Webster hosted a Grand Musical Entertainment and Fancy Dress Carnival. More than 100 carnival participants dressed in elaborate costumes marched from the U.S. Hotel to the Opera House accompanied by two bands. An audience of 800 people watched a medley of entertaining acts, and then danced until 4:30 AM.

At the close of the season, local events were often held at the theatre. In the spring of 1878 several school graduations, the Rugby Literary Society entertainment and the Millard Club Floral Concert were held. Wilmington High School's graduation was often held at the Opera House.

Fairs or bazaars frequently were set up in the theatre. The military fair held during the opening season was repeated during the 1872-1873 season. In December 1876 the Young Ladies Relief Society sponsored a three-day charity bazaar in the Opera House.

In December 1878 a Grand Bazaar was held for the benefit of the Provident Society of Wilmington. In 1877 the theatre housed a three-day art auction. Ravel's Gymnastic Acts, the Spelling Bees (particularly the Centennial Spelling Bee in 1875), and P. T. Barnum's troupe of Wild Indians were among the other novelties which attracted huge crowds.

Lectures

Each season numerous lectures were given to large audiences at the Opera House. John B. Gough, an inimitable story teller, appeared frequently and spoke on everything from *Peculiar People* to *Man and His Masters*. Mrs. Ann Eliza Young, nineteenth wife of Brigham Young, delivered a lecture entitled *My Life in Bondage*. Henry Ward Beecher lectured on *Hard Times*. Jonathan Byrne discussed *The Crusades and Their Influence upon Civilization*. Wong Chin Foo lectured on *China*. Other thought provoking addresses were entitled: *What shall we do with our daughters?*, *What a Man Owes to the Town he lives in*, and *The Escaped Nun*. During the 1880-1881 season the lectures were organized into the Diamond Course, a series of five lectures. The topics included *Great Deeds of Great Men, Heroes of the Homeric Age, The Probabilities of Life, Twenty Years After*, and readings by Professor Ralph Gibbard.

Lectures, which were an important source of education as well as entertainment, were so popular that by early 1878 the Masonic Hall Co. decided to convert the former Board of Trade rooms into a lecture room for smaller groups. Lectures were still given in the main hall, but talks on more limited topics could be given in the smaller room which rented for less money. Once the lecture room was opened during the 1878-1879 season, it hosted lectures as well as church meetings and concerts. During the first season the Millard Club, a local musical group, rented the hall for forty-three nights at a reduced rate. During the next season, the room was used for a variety of purposes, *e.g.*, Ogle's Rug Sale and the Mt. Vernon Ball. In the 1880s the lecture room became more commercial. Mr. Gillespie of Philadelphia rented the room for a dancing school in 1881. Mr. Worrell, a prime tenant, expanded his dry goods store into the lecture room in 1886.

PERFORMANCE INDEX*

*This is part of a complete performance index from 1872-1910 which, hopefully, will be published at some future date.

When the hall first opened no political meetings were permitted. However in August 1876 the Company reversed its decision and stated the hall could be rented for political meetings at $75 per night provided: "the money be paid before the gas is lit and some reliable person becoming responsible for any damage to the building or furniture."

Once the policy was changed, the theatre became an important meeting place. In the fall of election years, particularly the presidential election years of 1876, 1880, and 1884, numerous political meetings of both parties were held. The meetings were made more festive with various bands. On October 15, 1880 a grand meeting, "a credit to the democracy of Delaware," drew thousands of citizens to the theatre. Honorable Senator Thomas F. Bayard explained the tariff, "what it is and what it means," and urged each citizen to vote as a free man. According to the *Every Evening*:

the grand mass meeting was a credit to the democracy of Delaware . . . by 7:30 not an empty seat remained . . . audience of earnest, intelligent people, laborers, mechanics, merchants and manufacturers.[22]

A few days later 1,000 people attended the Republican meeting in which Senator Saulsbury discussed the issues of the campaign. The turnout for these political meetings was phenomenal. In describing the 1884 meetings reviewers speak of 1,500 people at the Democratic meetings and 2,000 people at the Young Men's Democratic Club. Temperance meetings and Y.M.C.A. meetings were also held with great frequency.

During the sixteen-year home management period, the Opera House was the center of drama, music, opera, minstrel shows, lectures, meetings, balls, fairs, and numerous other events. Innumerable questions arise: Why did melodrama enjoy such popularity?; What caused the intense heyday of opera?; Did Wilmington audiences follow the national norm in their tastes? At some later date, all of these questions must be explored, but the theme of *The Grand Experience* is more basic. Through its existence, the Grand Opera House made a rich diversity of entertainment experiences available to Delawarians for the first time. And as a catalyst it engendered

Outdoor stage at Brandywine Springs Park

the finest cultural events for some 40 years. From late August or September through May or June, the Opera House was the nucleus of entertainment. But in the summer all amusements were centered outside the city. There were excursions to Atlantic City, Cape May, and Coney Island. Concerts were scheduled in the parks. Outdoor summer entertainment continued as a common practice until the early 20th century. By the turn of the century, the new Brandywine Springs Park was the place to go.

Management

After hiring Mr. John H. Righter as theatre agent in 1873 the Masonic Hall Co. advertised that he was the only authorized agent to rent for concerts, lectures, operas, and dramatic performances. Mr. Righter only served until the end of 1874, when he was replaced by Mr. Jesse K. Baylis, who was theatre manager until 1888. Although Mr. Baylis was responsible for booking all events, the Hall Company still made all policy decisions. For instance, in 1879 the board voted to refuse the hall to all female minstrel groups. Mr.

83

James O'Neill in "The Count of Monte Cristo"

Baylis, who was well respected by the community, received credit
for many of the theatre's outstanding performances. In March 1886
Mr. Baylis arranged a performance of James O'Neill in *Monte
Cristo* as a benefit for himself. The *Every Evening* predicted that
the benefit would pack the theatre with Mr. Baylis' friends and
patrons. After the successful evening, the paper reported: "unique
in this city. It was the first time a benefit has ever been given to a
local manager . . . [a] step forward in dramatic matters." [23] Mr.

84

Baylis thanked the audience not only for the gratifying manifestation of interest in him and appreciation for his efforts, but for the spirit manifested throughout the evening to the play, players, and himself. So great was Mr. Baylis' popularity that, when the hall was leased to Proctor and Soulier, the newspaper announced Mr. Baylis would probably continue as local manager. In the meantime, Mr. Baylis and the Masonic Hall Company had a dispute, and Mr. Baylis was dismissed.

While Mr. Baylis was manager the Hall Co. usually did not discuss specific events, but it did devote much energy to making the theatre economically feasible. The fee schedule was continually adjusted in order to maximize the theatre's use. The initial fee schedule (theatrical events, $100; balls, $300; lectures, $60; concerts, $75; and Sunday School concerts $50) did not govern for long. During the initial season Mr. Ford had complained about the prices being high. By the fall of 1872, the second season, J. P. Allmond informed the board that according to other theatre managers, $100 a night was too high for drama, and the fee was reduced to $75. In the spring, the fee was raised back to $100 for the following season. The $100 fee would include one night's rental, two policemen, three ushers, a doorkeeper, and the necessary stage hands. Deductions of 10% would be given for three consecutive nights and of 15% for six consecutive nights. Before the fourth season, the price was lowered to $85 for one night and $80 for each succeeding night. In November 1875 the prices were lowered again to $75 for theatre and concerts, $175 for balls. Finally, in December 1876, because of the continued depression in business circles, the fee dropped to $60 except on holidays. In 1880 the fees were raised to $75 for theatricals, minstrel shows, and political meetings and $60 for concerts. These fees then remained static.

Since the Masons were anxious to make the theatre available, the Company generously granted reductions and rebates. The Washington Fire Co., which had paid $300 for their first ball, was charged $250 for the second and by 1875 only paid $225. In 1874, when the Young Ladies Relief Society proposed to rent the theatre for a performance which would be a benefit for the poor, the Masons lowered the rental fee to a minimal $30. Applications for fee reductions were constantly submitted to the board and were usually granted. Finally in the spring of 1881 the board decided to put an end to the requests by stating that all fees would be charged as announced.

Throughout the years of home management, the Hall Company managed the theatre with great economy. However, the receipts for the theatre averaged only about $6,768.25 per year. Only two dividends had been declared.

When the Academy of Music opened in 1886 the Opera House had serious competition. Although the Opera House maintained a full schedule of events, many of the best stars transferred to the Academy. Although the Masons stated that they wanted to maintain control of the theatre, they began to receive offers to rent the theatre. Eight months after the Academy of Music opened, John Smith (its lessee) offered to rent the Opera House but was declined. Finally in late 1887 a committee was appointed to consider the cost and method of running the auditorium "it being a matter of frequent discussion among the directors." In 1888, when the issue of a long term lease was being discussed, President Lobdell advised that by renting the hall on a long term basis and having the lessee pay some $3,000 in expenses, the Hall Co. might even increase its earnings. President Lobdell also assured the board that the character of performances would not hurt their reputation or be injurious to morals. President Lobdell claimed: "I do not think the character of performances would be more objectionable than they have been—could not be worse than last year—could not afford to be." He assured the board that it could prevent objectionable exhibitions and improper use of the house on Sunday.

In January 1888 a lease was formally signed with Proctor and Soulier, managers of the Academy of Music. Proctor and Soulier would pay $7,000 per year rent and would spend $10,000 in repairs during the first 5 years. Although Mr. Proctor had recently renewed his lease at the Academy of Music, he assured the Masonic Hall Company that he expected to close the Academy part of the time. According to the final terms of the lease, since none of the contemplated improvements would be made to the Academy of Music, it would virtually be closed. The new management would return the Grand Opera House to its unchallenged supremacy.

SCENE THREE

THE NATIONAL EXPERIMENT

1888-1890

F. F. Proctor, a former partner of H. R. Jacobs, controlled more theatres than almost any manager in the country. When he and his resident agent (Mr. Soulier) rented the Opera House, they made it a regular circuit stop. The increase in events was startling; over 200 events were held each season. The 1888-1889 season began with a flourish: more than forty unusually well attended events were held in September and October. *Dr. Jekyll and Mr. Hyde,* a dramatization of Stevenson's novel, played to packed houses. The Madison Square Company repeated *Jim the Penman* with its outstanding scenic effects to a large audience. The new management was praised for the efficient, capable orchestra which had been hired for the season.

Suddenly on October 23 at 8:30 PM the Academy of Music went up in flames. The mysterious fire caused great excitement in the community; thousands flocked to the ruins. Fortunately, no one had been in the building at the time of the fire. Mr. Soulier stated that the fire had probably started in the flies due to some electrical defect since two electric lights were burning. The City Electric Company denied this. An editorial urged the responsibility to be located so that those people using electricity could be relieved if the cause was not electrical. A great many people believed the "suspicious sounding fire" was of incendiary origin. The issue was never publically resolved; but both the Opera House and Proctor and Soulier benefited from the fire, since many of the best attractions were transferred to the Opera House and the rest were cancelled.

PERFORMANCE INDEX*

* This is part of a complete performance index from 1872-1910 which, hopefully, will be published at some future date.

1888 September

Yankee Moons and Bell Vivian:
Our Jonathan   1
Dore Davidson and Ramie Austin:
Dr. Jekyll and Mr. Hyde   3-5
Redmund & Barry Co.: Herminio
6-7
Thatcher, Primrose & West
Minstrels   8
Zitka   10-12
A Bunch of Keys   13-15
Monroe & Rice: My Aunt Bridget
24-26
McCarthy, McCall Co.: True Irish
Hearts   27-29

October

Sheffer & Blakley Refined Specialty
& Comedy Co.   1-3
Madison Square Theatre Co.: Jim
the Penman   4
The Kindergarten   5-6
Claire Scott: Mary Queen of Scots
9-10
Annie Berlein: Warning   11-13
Frank I. Frayne   15-17
Mardo   15
Si Slocum   16
Kentucky Bill   17
Simmons & Donnelly Co.: Fashions
2
Fleming's Co.: Around the World in
80 Days   22-24
Ollie Redpath & Co.: Pert, also
Russian Prestidigitateurs   25-27
Francis Redding: An Oath to the
Dead   29-30
The Octoroon and Rose Cottage   31

November

Francis Redding: "Nobody's Child
2-3
Francis Redding: Maritana   3
Miaco's Pantomime Co.: Magic
Talisman   6-8
Ten Nights in a Bar Room   8-10
Miss Jeannie Winston, 7 Lyceum
Opera Co.   12-14
Grand Duchess   12
Girofle-Girofla   13
Fra Diavola and Grand Duchess
14
Irwin Bros. Specialty Show   15-17
Hardee & Von Leer: On the Frontier
22-24
A Night in Jersey   20-21
Zo-Zo the Magic Queen   26-28
Over the Garden Wall   29-30

December

Over the Garden Wall   1
Twelve Temptations   3

Arthur Rehan's Co.: Nancy & Co.
4-5
7-20-8   5
Beacon Lights   6-8
Charles T. Ellis: Casper the Yodler
10-12
The American Opera Co.: Daughter
of the Regiment   13-14
American Opera Co.: Maritana and
Faust   14
Uncle Tom's Cabin   15
Wilbur Opera Co.   17-21
The Merry War   17
The Princess of Trebimonde   18
The Mascott   19
The Two Vagabonds   20
Three Black Cloaks   21
Johnson & Slavin Minstrels   22
Two Johns   24-26
Dowling & Hasson: Nobody's Claim
27-29
Jule Keane: Only a German   31

1889 January

Jule Keane: Only a German   1-2
Duff Opera Co.: Queen's Mate   3-4
Mother Goose   5
Jonathan Wild: Running Wild   7
McNish, Ranza & Arno's Minstrels
8
Choral Club of Wilmington: Pirates
of Penzance   9-10
Barry & Fay McKenna's Flirtation
11-12
Floy Crowell   14-19
Infatuation   14
Ingomar   15
Jess   16
May Blossom   17
A Hoop of Gold   18
Infatuation   19
One of the Finest   21-23
Lyceum Opera Co., Miss Jeannie
Winston   24-26
Boccacio   24
La Perichole   25
Fra Diavolo and Boccacio   26
Keep It Dark   28-30
Miss Lee Lamar: Fate   31

February

Fate   1-2
Pat Rooney: Pat's Wardrobe   4-6
May Howard & Burlesque Co.   8-9
Miss Minnie Dupree & Co.   11-16
Held by the Enemy   11-13
My Partner   14-16
Dockstader's Ministrels   18
One of the Bravest   19-2
Santley Female Burlesques   21-23
Frank Kilday's Co.: The Streets of
New York   25-27
Halien & Hart: Later On   28

March

Later On   1
Mme. Bishop Shakespearian College
of Philadelphia: Caste   2
Leavitt's Folly & Burlesque Co.   4-6
Walter S. Sanford: Under the Lash
7-9
Australian Novelty Co.   11-13
C. W. Coulcock Co.: Hazel Kirke
14-16
Jennie Calef   18-20
Kathleen Mavourneen   18
An American Princess   18-2
Fanchon the Cricket   19
Little Barefoot   20
The Paymaster   21-23
The Night Owls Specialty &
Burlesque Co.   25-31

April

Hettie Bernard Chase: The Little
Coquette   1-3
Atkinson's Comedy Co.: Peck's Bad
Boy   4-6
Thatcher, Primrose and West's
Minstrels   8
Henry E. Dixey & Comedy Co.:
Adonis   9
Marie Wainwright & Louis James:
Othello   10
Stanley Macey: C.O.D.   15-18
Johnathan Wild: Running Wild
19-20
Kiralfy's Water Queen   22
Lillie Clay's Gaiety Co.   23
Juch-Perotti Concert   24
Mr. Aiden Benedect: Monte Cristo
25-27
Kellar, Magician   29-30

May

Kellar, Magician   1
Lotta: Musette   2
Lyceum Theatre Co.: The Wife   3
College of Music Cantata: The
Cadet's Picnic   6
Miss Jarbeau: Starlight   7-8
Tony Pastor Troupe   9-11
E. P. Sullivan: A Celebrated Case
13-14
Mr. McKee Rankin: The Runaway
Wife   15
Fanny Davenport: Tosca   18
E. P. Sullivan & Co.: A Celebrated
Case   20-22
Miss May Treat: Ranch King
30-31

June

Miss May Treat: Ranch King   1
Tuesday Club Floral Concert   4
Choral Club: Bohemian Girl   12

The overwhelming majority of performances still fell into the dramatic category. Troupes were in residence for three days and gave four performances: Monday, Tuesday, Wednesday matinée and evening—or Thursday, Friday, Saturday matinée and evening. Serious drama still failed to draw the public. When *Nancy and Company,* a clean, straight, elevating dramatic work, was presented, audiences failed to support. But *Twelve Temptations,* a "tedious, tiresome, disappointing spectacle" drew a huge assemblage and was the success of the 1888-1889 season. Many of the old favorites—Fanny Davenport, Lotta, and Annie Pixley still appeared. The big change in dramatic performances was the marked increase in vaudeville and burlesque performances. After a performance by the May Howard and Burlesque Company, the *Every Evening* commented:

the performance or that part which presented the bit burlesquers in their anatomical development seemed to meet with the hearty appreciation of the audience.[1]

Later in the season in April a performance of *Othello* drew a small crowd, while the Henry E. Dixey Burlesque and Comedy Co. drew a capacity audience. With a note of disdain, the critics stated:

Burlesquer Dixey is a bigger man than the late Bard of Avon in the appreciation of Wilmington playgoers. Adonis and its pretty girls in tights packed the Opera House while Shakespeare at usual prices had only a fair sized audience.[2]

After the "most notable dramatic event of the season" (Madame Janauschek in *Meg Merrille* on November 1889) was attended by a large audience, a local critic disdainfully suggested:

the presence of a large audience should be sufficient encouragement to the management to bring more first class plays to this community which has been surfeited with poor burlesque and pieces of "horse play" orders.[3]

Few professional musical concerts were given, The Ringgold Band concert was one, but local groups like the Choral Club of Wilmington performed several times. True to its form of supporting local groups, the most fashionable audience of the season did support the Floral Concert by the Tuesday Club on June 4, 1889. One critic suggested that the public's lack of appreciation for music was based on the scarcity of good music:

it is regrettable that the people of Wilmington do not have more chance to hear good music well rendered . . . musical taste of Wilmington audiences would improve more rapidly with frequent hearing of classical music.[4]

Several popular minstrel troupes continued to appear. Popular operas were presented by the Lyceum Opera Co. and the Wilbur Opera Company. Grand opera performed by the American Opera Co., the Dugg Opera Co., and the Juch Perotti troupe failed to draw support. Kellar the magician and Bartholew's Equine Paradox were among the popular variety show attractions. One innovation was to have the election returns read from the stage in November 1888.

Despite their high hopes when they assumed management of the Opera House, by the spring of the second season Proctor and Soulier realized that the Opera House could not support a full calendar of events like other circuit theatres. They were continually taking receipts from other theatres and putting them into the sinking fund in Wilmington. In an attempt to lower the rent and their losses they wrote in a letter of May 2, 1890:

having been in the city 2 years, in view of the limited number of theatre going public, of the expense attached and of near at hand opposition and the fact that we have already lost $3,500 in the present season, plus you know what the first season was, we say it is impossible for us to pay more than $5,000 per year commencing September 1 next.

At first the board refused to accept the offer, but after several months of bargaining the two parties did agree on a yearly rent of $5,500. Although Proctor and Soulier agreed to the new terms, by November they had not paid the amount due and the Hall Company was forced to legally repossess the theatre. As soon as they regained possession of the hall in November, the Masons returned to a system of home management and hired Mr. Williamson as theatre manager. Mr. Williamson gave public notice of the change in management.

The short lived era as a circuit theatre had ended in failure. Wilmington audiences patronized events according to their own eclectic tastes and would not accept every attraction selected by a national team. Burlesque and cheap melodramas were simply not acceptable to the majority of the Wilmington theatre going public. Perhaps there really was such a phenomenon as the Wilmington taste.

GRAND OPERA HOUSE

Wm. R. WILLIAMSON, Sole Mgr.

WILMINGTON, DEL.

SEASON OF 94-95.

GEO. A. WOLF DES. WILMINGTON DEL.

VOL. VI.   WEEK ENDING MARCH 16, 1895.   No. 138.

PICKINGS.

The Labor Question—Is it near 12 o'clock, boss.

Wear Monarch Shirts—Sold by all leading furnishers.

The Chicago aristocrat is a real lard of creation.

Monarch Shirts are the best made. Try them and be convinced.

School Teacher—Can you tell me from which city we obtain most of our pork?

Class (in chorus)—Chic-hog-o!

Monarch Shirts are guaranteed goods. If your furnisher doesn't keep them, write us, we'll tell you lots who do.

Maud—Is Mr. Merton still paying attention to your daughter?

Mr. Goldbug—Why, gracious, no! He's not paying her any attention at all now. They're married.

Gabriel—The new arrival is a New Yorker.

St. Peter—How do you know?

Gabriel—He arrived here Sunday morning and gave three raps on the side door.

Monarch Shirts will fit you. Try them!

Reary Raggles—Got any terbacker. Dusty?

Dusty Rhoades—Nuff for one chew.

Reary Raggles—Let's chuck up ter see who get's it.

Dusty Rhoades—Wot's ther use. I know I've got it and you know you haint.

Arrow Brand Collars fit Monarch Shirts, and Monarch Shirts will fit you. Try them.

Willie—Got a new Sunday school teacher, but I don't like him.

Father—Why so, my son?

Willie—He's the butcher and he talked shop all afternoon.

Father (surprised)—Why, what do you mean, Willie?

Willie—Why he talked about killing the fatted calf, and led like a lamb to the slaughter.

Fit, finish, fabric and fashion are perfect in Monarch Shirts.

Visitor—Have you any relics of the last battle fought here?

Storekeeper—Why, certainly, sir. Just wait one minute.

Storekeeper (speaking down tube)—John, mould about twenty bullets, and have the blacksmith hammer out a bayonet in a hurry.

Have you tried Monarch Shirts?

There is a ladies' toilet room to the left of the foyer, where a maid will be in attendance during each entertainment.

Wraps, umbrellas, etc., can be checked in the lobby.

Tickets can be ordered by mail, telegraph or telephone No. 518.

THE WILMINGTON CITY ELECTRIC CO.

ARC LIGHTS.   INCANDESCENT LIGHTS.   MOTIVE POWER.

The Best is the Cheapest Light.

FIND YOUR **FORTUNE** IN LUCKY

SANTO DOMINGO.

Investment bonds guaranteed by the **Santo Domingo Guaranty Co.**

Allotments take place monthly, and are payable in U. S. gold coin in sums of **$160,000, $40,000, $20,000,** etc.

5,692 Bonds paid monthly, aggregating **$574,880.** Subscription fees, **$10, $5, $2, $1, 50c.** and **25c.**

Apply to Local Agents, or address,

ANTONIO MORA, City of Santo Domingo, Santo Domingo.

A. L. AINSCOW & CO.'S

TELEPHONE 657.

CAFÉ,

802 MARKET AND 109 EAST FOURTH STREET.

WILMINGTON'S DELMONICO.

THEATRE PARTIES A SPECIALTY.   PRIVATE DINING ROOMS.

Choicest grades of OYSTERS.   FUR, FIN AND FEATHER IN SEASON.

NONPAREIL STEAM LAUNDRY,

503 SHIPLEY STREET.

BEST FACILITIES, consequently finest work. We know our business thoroughly and guarantee you satisfaction. The finest blanket as well as the richest lace curtain properly treated.

PHONE 764.

MISS ALICE M. BOYLE, Manager.

Cummings

The Photographer,

302 Market St.,

WILMINGTON, DEL.

PROGRAM.

SATURDAY EVENING, MARCH 16th.

MARIE TAVARY

Grand Opera Co.

CHARLES H. PRATT, Proprietor and Manager.

(Continued on 2d and 3d pages.)

WILMINGTON CANDY CO.

HAS REMOVED

TO

224 MARKET STREET.

The James & Webb Building.

"THE MINT,"

JAMES P. HASSON, Proprietor,

NO. 813 MARKET STREET.

FINE WINES AND LIQUORS.

Electric Connection with Opera House Stage.

FOR SALE BY ALL FIRST-CLASS GROCERS.

R. G. SMITH & CO.,

WHOLESALE AGENTS,

236 E. LIBERTY STREET.

HARRY W. LOWE,

Livery and Boarding Stables,

323 to 327 EAST THIRD ST.

Fine Coaches for Weddings, Balls, Parties, etc.

TELEPHONE, NO. 10.

Herring-Hall-Marvin Co.

SAFES

.....ARE THE BEST.

FACTORIES:

Cincinnati, New York, Philadelphia.

PERFORMANCE INDEX*

*This is part of a complete performance index from 1872-1910 which, hopefully, will be published at some future date.

SCENE FOUR

THE MULTIFACETED HOUSE

1890-1904

The disappointing years of national management had not helped the image of theatre in Delaware. In 1891 an irate stockholder sent a letter to the *Every Evening* in which he suggested the theatre be done away with:

as it is an annoyance to the fraternity, and the King Street front be leveled with the street and be used as a market house or for some other business. Let Pillars be erected from the cellar to support the rooms above and the second and third floors be put in with an elevator, using one floor for a lecture room and the balance for offices . . . I believe this could be done without much expense and it would bring in a larger revenue than it ever has as a theatre.[1]

The anonymous stockholder also criticized the financial management: the lack of dividends after 20 years, the loss of surety of the last lessee, and the fact that the expenses were double what they had been under Mr. Baylis.

Aware of his opposition, Manager Williamson often emphasized the chief objective of the theatre—to maintain cleanliness. At the beginning of the third season Mr. Williamson stated explicitly:

the distinctive object has always been and will continue to be kept in view —the presentation of entertainments that are clean in every sense of that much abused word. Attractions may and of course will vary in their stature of their artistic and literary worth but patrons of the house may rely with the most positive assurance upon always witnessing representations whether dramatic, operatic, comedy or farce that are thoroughly fit for the eyes and ears of women and children.[2]

By 1895 relations between Mr. Williamson and the Hall Co. had deteriorated. Believing that Mr. Williamson had lost respect for the orders of the board, the Hall Co. demanded his resignation. In August 1895 the Company signed a lease with Mr. Baylis, the former manager, who continued to lease the hall until 1904.

During this 14-year period, the Opera House maintained its status as Wilmington's major theatre, despite the existence of other theatres, and it continued to present a wide variety of entertainment.

During the years of Mr. Williamson's management, the number of performances per year decreased from a high of 180 in 1890 to a low of 140 in 1894-1895. Mr. Baylis began with a limited program of 125 events, but he increased the performance level until at the turn of the century there were nearly 250 events a season.

Etta Reed

Dramatic

The largest number of attractions continued to fall in the dramatic category. At the beginning of the 1890s the dramatic performances account for more than half of the total events. The percentage of dramatic performances continually increased until by the 1897-1898 season they account for more than 85% of all performances. The increase in dramatic performances was due to the presence of numerous traveling companies which arrived in Wilmington for week-long stays. During their residence the companies usually performed every evening and nearly every afternoon.

One of the earliest of these troupes was the Waite Comedy Company. In 1893-1894 the company performed every evening from Monday, March 19 to Saturday, March 24 with a change of play at every performance. The plays, offered at the popular prices of ten and twenty cents, included: *Mazie the Romp, Legally Dead, Young America, The Man from Catterugus,* and *Rip Van Winkle.*

The Waite Company continued to be a Wilmington favorite. In January 1897, when the Company was in residence for a week, it presented one play at the matinée and a different attraction in the evening. In one week ten different plays, including *A Lady of Lyon, Kathleen Mauvoreen,* and Frohman's *Lost Paradise* were performed. After several successful performances the *Every Evening* critic commented: "The Waite Comedy Co. has simply taken the town by storm. The matinées crowd the house as well as the night performances."[3] During the 1897-1898 season, the company was in residence from November 8-20 and performed twenty-two times in more than eleven different plays.

The Corse Payton troupe became another Wilmington favorite. When Mr. Corse Payton, accompanied by Miss Etta Reed, performed in Wilmington in August 1898, their performances were so successful that they extended their residence for a second week. After two successful performances on Wednesday, August 31 of *Camille* and *My Old Kentucky Home* the *Every Evening* reported:

Notwithstanding the counter attractions of the park and excursions yesterday, there wasn't the slightest falling off in Corse Payton's audiences at the Grand Opera House. At the matinee over 1200 people . . . At night the war play "My Old Kentucky Home" drew a crowded house. All enjoyed the patriotic speeches and the comedy work of Mr. Payton so completely that cheers and laughter reigned supreme.[4]

Robert Mantell appeared frequently at The Grand Opera House

During the second week some of the best loved plays like *Jim the Penman, Camille,* and *The Galley Slave* were repeated, but different plays were added to the repertoire.

The troupe reappeared during Christmas week—traditionally a heavy theatre-going time—with other selections. On Christmas Day 1898 the matinée (*On the Rappahannock*) and the evening performance (*Woman Against Women*) broke all records:

The house was crowded to its greatest capacity at both performances but the number of people turned away particularly at night was remarkable, nothing like it having been experienced before. But the capacity of the house was exhausted and there was no help for it.[5]

The Corse Payton Company which was "welcome everywhere it appeared," continued to perform every season. The repertoire was always expanding, and the newest entertainment ideas were incorporated. During their residence in February 1903 the company scored a great hit with picture songs in which words were projected on the canvas by lanterns so that the audience could join in chorus.

Some of the other troupes which frequented the Opera House around the turn of the century were: The Spooners, Elroy's Stock Company, the King Dramatic Company, the Ideals, the Bennett & Moulton Co., Chester de Vonde & Co., Katherine Rober & Co., and Thomas Shea and Co. Each troupe was in residence for at least a week and provided a variety of plays at matinée and evening performances. One wonders how the multitude of performances continually attracted audiences.

Many dramatic events came to the Opera House as single billings. Charles Frohman, one of the most popular producers of the late 19th century, often brought his stock company to the Grand Opera House. *Shenandoah,* the play which established Mr. Frohman's reputation, was performed at the Opera House in November 1890. During the 1892-1893 season Frohman's company appeared three times in February in *His Wedding Day, The Lost Paradise* (an American labor play by H. C. DeMille), and *Gloriana.* In April the company returned to perform Belasco and DeMille's play *Men and Women.* Frohman's *Jane,* "a comedy which bubbled over with mirth," was repeated numerous times over the years. The play, which had been a great New York success, was labelled the "prime favorite play" of the theatregoers.

The Count of Monte Cristo, which had first been performed as a benefit for Mr. Baylis, was another Wilmington favorite. The play, which became one of the great successes of the American stage, featured James O'Neill, the father of Eugene O'Neill, in the title rôle. *Darkest Russia*, a drama which was labelled the "finest dramatic construction seen on the stage for years," was repeated at least once a season and often more.

During the 1890s Charles Hoyt's comedies, which directly influenced modern musical comedy, were produced very frequently. One of the favorites was *A Bunch of Keys,* a satire on hotels. Labelled a musical comedy in three acts, it abounded with humor from the opening note, which explained why the play was called comedy:

comedy is the word used to describe almost everything put upon the stage at present and the author's desire to avoid the charge of eccentricity having enough else to answer for . . .[6]

The final performance of the 1896-1897 season was a performance of Hoyt's play, *A Contented Woman,* which drew a capacity crowd: "every seat in the house was sold sometime in advance and standing room was being bought at 8 o'clock." [7] During the 1898-1899 season four different Hoyt comedies were performed: *A Parlor's March, A Stranger in New York, A Bunch of Keys,* and *A Milk White Flag.* A pantomime of *Ben Hur* drew capacity crowds at its performances on February 22, 23, and 25 in 1895.

The interest in drama was so strong that in 1889 a local acting club was organized and made its debut at Eden Hall. The club, which became known as the Wilmington Dramatic Club, acquitted itself so creditably that it moved to the Grand Opera House in January 1891 for a performance of *Snowed In.* It continued to perform at the Opera House throughout the decade. During the 1890s, thirtieth production, *Married Life* on May 31, 1899, was a commemorative occasion.

Old favorites Ann Pixley, Frank Mayo, Joe Jefferson, Lotta, John Drew, and James O'Neill continued to appear along with new stars Thomas Shea, Chester de Vonde, Marie Frohman, and Clara Morris.

SOUVENIR PROGRAM·

10TH SEASON 98-99·

MARRIED LIFE

GRAND OPERA HOUSE

WILMINGTON DELAWARE MAY 31ST

30th Performance

Variety programs retained their appeal. Gus Hill and his New York Vaudeville Stars was one of the most popular during the early years. During the 1900-1901 season J. K. Burke's festivals of vaudeville, which combined famous actors and troupes with novelty events, was presented three times in one season. The program on October 4, 1894 featured Charles T. Ellis (of *Caspar the Yodler* fame) in a brief dramatic piece, the Milton Aborn Comedy Co., as well as violinists and acrobats. Burlesque never played a large rôle at the Opera House, but M. B. Leavitt, who originated burlesque as Americans know it, always had several plays in Wilmington. *The Spider and the Fly* was a great hit at the Opera House. The play was a musical farce which used sixty people from both continents as well as elaborate scenery and electric effects.

99

Another frequent attraction was the Byrne Brothers in *Eight Bells,* a mixture of comedy and pantomime. The four brothers who were comedians and acrobatic artists gave a performance filled with "mirthful situations and climaxes that threw the audience into convulsions."

Uncle Tom's Cabin continued to appear frequently. Since there were always some people who had not seen the play, it continued to draw enthusiastic response. During a performance of the play in September 1900 one member of the audience became so engrossed in the action he became quite vocal. He "resent[ed] Simon LeGree's cruelty to Uncle Tom and when the latter was knocked down by LeGree shouted, Get up and punch him, Tom." [8]

While the number of dramas far overpowered all other productions, the theatre did continue to provide diversified entertainment.

Minstrel Shows

Minstrel troupes performed numerous times each season before large audiences. Lew Dockstader, Primroe & West, and Al G. Fields were among the favorites. Minstrelsy was so popular that Wilmington even formed its own minstrel company in 1889 in order to play small towns in the vicinity. On February 1, 1894 the Wilmington Minstrels, an amateur organization with unusual merit, gave a fine programme at the Opera House. The reviewer claimed that despite the use of exclusively local talent, "all performers acquitted themselves in a creditable manner."

Opera

Comic opera was enormously popular during these years. The most popular comic opera at the Grand was *Wang,* nationally heralded as the greatest of comic opera successes. The opera glistened with royal magnificence. At the 1896 performance Albert Hart was the King of Siam and the company had all new costumes and scenery. In order to emphasize the "gorgeousness" of the opera, the *Every Evening* explained that 100 costumes were used by the chorus alone.

Right: "Wang"—a Comic Opera

When the Digby Bell Comic Opera Company performed *Tar and Tartar* on September 25, 1893 the audience was in a constant roar of laughter. The opera was repeated by several other companies, including the Bijou Opera Co. and the Waite Comic Opera Co. *Maritana,* one of the numerous performances by the Waite Comic Opera Co., was praised as one of the best performances ever given in this city. The presentation of the Waite Company's new opera *Paul Jones* on January 24, 1898 drew a full house: "filled to over-flowing—one of the most fashionable audiences of the season and all present were highly pleased." [9]

Grand opera was also performed. On March 16, 1985 the Grand English Opera Co. performed *Cavalleria Rusticana* and *I'Pagliacci.* Milton Aborn's New England Opera Co. made numerous visits to the Opera House. Another popular troupe was the Wilbur Opera Co. which drew large crowds when it introduced dime matinées. Given the enthusiastic response to opera, local talent gathered together and formed the Wilmington Opera Club. On May 22 and 23, 1895 the club performed *Mikado* at the Opera House. The gala event under the direction of T. Leslie Carpenter was well received: "in regard to the chorus and general music work, there was evidence everywhere of marked improvement in the work." [10]

Concerts became a more popular form of entertainment. A large, enthusiastic audience attended a Strauss concert on October 13, 1890. Among the big band concerts that drew enthusiastic response was John Philip Sousa and his band, which performed numerous times between 1892 and the early years of the 20th century. Although the crowd at the October 30, 1893 concert was not very large, the performance turned into a happening:

. . . the music enthralled the whole audience. It leaped from the point of Sousa's wand and thrilled listeners, whose eyes followed the swaying, the swinging. . . . But when Sousa gave the introductory notes of Washington Post (his own great composition) before one bar had been finished, the house, to use a phrase, got into it and a thunder of applause broke out. This was the personal compliment Wilmington was going to give the Master and he bowed and bowed and the cheers continued.[11]

At the April 24, 1899 matinée Sousa's musicians received a warm welcome, every number being loudly encored.

Right: A rare program of a Sousa Concert discovered in the restoration of The Grand Opera House

SOUSA
AND
HIS
BAND

GRAND OPERA HOUSE

WILMINGTON

Afternoon only, Friday, April 21

SOUSA AND HIS BAND.

Miscellaneous

From high music to high trapeze, the Opera House was never limited. Athletic performances became increasingly popular throughout the period. The Warren Athletic Club presented three exhibitions of boxing, wrestling, and gymnastic feats in the 1891-1892 season alone. The Diamond State Athletic Association, Delaware's contribution to the athletic field, performed musical and athletic feats. After a very successful boxing entertainment in January 1895, the Association was given the supreme compliment: "one of the finest of the kind ever given . . . reminded lovers of sparring exhibitions of the Warren Club days."

The moving picture began innocently enough as an added attraction to live performances. On October 12, 1896 a program featuring hypnotists X. Lamotte Sage and Olga Helen Sage also included Lumière's Cinematographe. On April 13 and 14, 1900, pictures of the Jeffries-Sharkey fight were shown. In 1903 the Corse Peyton Co. presented song slides as an added attraction. Despite the fact that one full leigth film, *"The Entire Passion Play,"* was shown on April 9, 1903, the movies were still basically a bonus attraction. They soon grew to enormous and devastating proportions.

Meeting Place

The Grand Opera House maintained its rôle as an important meeting house. Political meetings, which would attract large crowds, were often held during presidential election years. In November 1892 Senator Bayard addressed a large audience. On election night, the returns were broadcast at the theatre. As part of a day-long conference on temperance on March 23, 1892 Elizabeth Greenwood, national superintendent of the Women's Christian Temperance Union, spoke at the Opera House. The auditorium was filled to capacity: "every seat was occupied and many were forced to stand throughout the whole of the services." [12]

Meetings of general interest which would attract large audiences were held at the Opera House. In April 1903, there were mass riots against the Jews in Kishineff, southern Russia. When news of the outrages reached the United States, public manifestations of sympathy began throughout the country. "Day by day for almost two months thereafter the people of the United States created opportunities for expressing their indignation through mass meetings, sermons, editorials and resolutions." In Wilmington the protest took the form of a mass meeting held at the Opera House on June 1, 1903. The crowd filled the theatre to overflowing. Numerous leading Delawarians, including Governor Hunn, Judge George Gray, Postmaster Heald, and members of City Council were present. Governor Hunn introduced the meeting by claiming such a state of affairs could only be brought about by fanaticism and ignorance. Mr. Bernard Harris of Philadelphia gave a brief address. He was followed by the principal speaker, George Gray, the outstanding Delaware statesman who almost became the Democratic candidate for President. Judge Gray delivered an eloquent address which chastized the Czars for the loathsome deeds that had occurred:

I am here to voice what I believe to be the universal sentiment of Christian America, the universal sentiment of American citizenship throughout the length and breadth of this broad land of ours—sentiments of sympathy for the suffering men, women and children who have survived this horror, sympathy with you who are of their race and blood, and of protest to be uttered by this great nation, of which we are a part, against the horror and the perfidy and the outrage of the whole matter.[13]

Throughout the speech there were cheers and sighs.

During thirty-three years the Grand Opera House maintained its rank as Delaware's outstanding theatre by carefully mixing the old favorites with current developments in entertainment: resident comedy companies, comic operas, and moving pictures. In other words management adapted the theatre to the times. The diversity of events, which was planned to meet the Delaware audience's desires, included attractions for every taste.

PERFORMANCE INDEX*

* This is part of a complete performance index from 1872-1910 which, hopefully, will be published at some future date.

1907 August
The Mayor of Loughland   19
Montana   31

September
The King Bee   2-3
Williams & Walker: Bandana Land   4
Zira   6
Nixon and Zimmerman Revival:
   Miss Bob White   7
The Lion and the Mouse   9-10
Lillian Blauvelt: Dream City   14
Nixon & Zimmerman: Simple Simon
   Simple   17
Judith of the Plains   18
Paul Gilmore: The Wheel of Love
   19
Nixon & Zimmerman: Gingerbread
   Man   21
Done Brown   23
John Griffith: King Richard III   25
The Lost Trail   27

October
Joseph and William Jefferson: The
   Rivals   2
The Road to Yesterday   3
The Spring Chicken   4
The Step-sister   5
Kirke La Shelle Co.: The Virginian
   7
Mr. Blue Beard   8
Grace Cameron: Little Dolly
   Dimples   9
The Reformation or The Life of
   Martin Luther   10-11
The Skating Rink Girl   12
Earl Burgess Company   14-19
   Wedded and Parted   14
   Her Life or His and The Ranch
      King   15
   The Ranch King and Ruined
      Lives   16
   Runied Lives and Human Spiders
      17
   Human Spiders and Libley Prison
      18
   A Bowery Boy and Fighting the
      Flames   19
Mass Meeting: Temperance & Order
   vs. Prohibition & Disorder   23
Carlotta Willson: The Three of Us
   24
George M. Cohan: George

Washington, Jr.   25
A Warm Match   28

November
Shore Acres   1
Nat C. Goodwin Co.: In Mizzoura
   2
Tom Miner's Bohemian Burlesquer's
   4-6
The Dreamland Burlesquer's   11-13
Philadelphia Orchestra   14
Sam & Lee Shubert: The Truth   15
Blanche Walsh & Astor Theatre Co.:
   The Straight Road   16
Jan Paderewski, Pianist   20
Charles Frohman: The Dairyman
   23
Buster Brown   25
London Gaiety Girls: Mixing
   Things Up   28-30

December
What Women Will Do   2
Wilmington Orchestra   3
Lew Dockstader's Minstrels   6
A Pair of Country Kids   7
Murray & Maskey Comedy Co.
   9-12
   A Prisoner of War   9
   Lost to the World   10
   The Shadow Detective and The
      Will-O-Wisp   11
   Dr. Jekyll & Mr. Hyde   12
Philadelphia Orchestra   19
Henry Miller: The Great Divide
   25
Harry Webber: Nip & Tuck   30
Promenade Concert & Dance   31

1908 January
The Passion Play   1
San Carlo Opera Co.: La Traviata
   8
Philadelphia Orchestra   9
Poor Relation   11
Quincy Adams Sawyer   13-18
Eddie Fay: The Orchid   25

February
Inaugural of the Season's Earthwide
   Moving Pictures: 1
   The Merry Widow, Ben
   Hur, The Prodigal Son, The
   Great Thaw Trial, The
   Passion Play, Eight comedy
   pictures

His Honor, The Mayor   3
The Chicken Trust   5
Sam and Lee Shubert: A Village
   Lawyer   7
Al G. Field's Minstrels   8
My Mamie Rose   11
Philadelphia Orchestra   13
Leo Ditrichstein & Co.: Bluffs   22

March
Wilmington Orchestra Concert   3
Ethel Barrymore: Her Sister   6
John W. Vogel's Big City Minstrels
   18
Porter Waite: Faust   19
Helen Grayce & Co.   23-28
   The Pride of Jennico   23
   The Little Minister and When
      We Were Twenty-One   24
   Thelma and In the Palace of the
      King   25
   Romeo and Juliet and In the
      Bishops Carriage   26
   When We Were Twenty-One and
      The Pit   27
   In the Palace of the King and
      The Christian   28
Under Southern Skies   31

April
Charles Frohman Presents Marie
   Doro: The Morals of Marcus
   4
Frohman Presents Hattie Williams:
   The Little Cherub   8
Harry Kelley: His Honor, The
   Mayor   13
The Man of the Hour   18
The Red Mill   20
Mme. Nazimova: A Doll's House
   23
Lillian Nordica, Walter Damrosch,
   and the New York Symphony
   Orchestra   24
Delaware Saengerbund Concert   27

May
The Hayden   1
Wilmington Orchestra Concert   5
New York Star Vaudeville Co.
   19-20
Miss McClafferty's Dancing School's
   Annual May Carnival   21

SCENE FIVE

NATIONAL MANAGEMENT - A TRANSITION

The final transition of the Grand Opera House from legitimate theatre to vaudeville house to movie theatre occurred between 1904 and 1910 under national management. When Mr. Baylis was not able to continue his lease, Nixon and Zimmerman, managing agents who were part of a national syndicate, assumed management and immediately cut the number of performances. The performance level dropped to some 120 events a year.

After just two seasons as managers, during the summer of 1906, Fred G. Nixon Niedlinger found it necessary to ask for a reduction in rent. Echoing F. F. Proctor's words of 1888, he claimed that the theatre was losing money and explained:

... would like to continue as tenants but want some concessions. The Wilmington proposition has cost us during the last 2 years between $5,000 and $7,000 though we still have confidence in the town and would like to continue if you are a little liberal in treatment.

Better terms were arranged and the Nixon-Zimmerman partnership continued as lessee. However, they seem to have lost interest in the theatre, the number and caliber of events began to decline.

Dramatic

Although dramatic performances were still the major form of entertainment, the severe decline in the number of comedy companies who were in residence greatly reducd the number of performances per season. The Thomas Shea Company, the Chester de Vonde and the Corse Payton Company were among the few that still appeared. Most dramas were produced just one or twice.

Famed Joseph Jefferson appeared in *The Rivals* in October 1907, and the pleasure of the audience was demonstrated by frequent applause. Ethel Barrymore appeared during the 1904-1905 season in *Sunday* and in the 1907-1908 season in *Sister*. The appearance of Lionel Barrymore in *The Other Girl* in January 1905 turned into a slight disaster. Because of a railroad blockade, the company barely managed to reach Wilmington:

Ethel Barrymore

The scenery and costumes were lost on the line somewhere between this city and Harrisburg. Many people were disappointed at the unfortunate failure but it could not be helped.[1]

Charles Frohman's plays were produced frequently. *Romeo and Juliet* on February 13, 1905 was fully appreciated by a large audience: "nearly 4 hours but it was a continuous presentation of such beautiful stage settings and perfect acting that not a minute of the time proved tedious to the large audience present."[2] *Uncle Tom's Cabin* and *Black Crook* were still popular. Hoyt's comedies drew large crowds. Nixon Zimmerman brought in several of their productions: *Gingerbread Man, The Office Boy*, and *Simple, Simon, Simple.*

Concerts

The biggest change at the Opera House was the warm reception now afforded to serious music. Throughout the 19th century concerts were infrequently held and were poorly received. When the Philadelphia orchestra first began performing in 1901 audiences were often small, but the crowd quickly built up. By the 1905-1906 season the concerts had become so popular that a Wilmington series of three concerts was inaugurated under the direction of conductor Fritz Scheel. The Philadelphia Orchestra's Wilmington series, was an unbroken tradition until 1913. By the 1907-1908 season the series was under the new conductor, Carl Pohlig. The December 19 concert, featuring soloist Britt, was a huge success; but regulations like today forbid an encore. According to reports:

the soloist Mr. Britt received an ovation well deserved for his playing of the concerto. In all the applause for this and other numbers there was felt a desire for an encore or the same selection over and over again, but the printed rule was rigidly observed.[3]

By the 1909-1910 season the series had a large following. The January concert was attended by an appreciative audience, and the feeling appeared to be that the concert was the best of the present series. The concert was longer than usual; it began promptly at 8:30 PM and did not end until 10:15.

An exciting feature of the series was that the audience was given a chance to select the final program. At the January concert the audience was reminded to "give the ballot to the usher when leaving the theatre." The votes resulted in a fine classical program at the February concert which included: Mendelssohn's overture *A Midsummer Night's Dream*, Tschaikovsky's *Symphonie Pathétique*, Greig's *Suite Opus 16*, and Wagner's *Overture Tannhauser*. After the request concert a reception was given for conductor Pohlig and members of the orchestra.

The response to other musical events indicates that the appreciation of serious music had increased. On November 20, 1907 the famous pianist Jan Paderewski played before an audience which crowded the house and listened with rapt attention. After the Schubert Liszt selection he was presented with a huge bunch of red and white roses tied with streamers of ribbon of corresponding colors. On

April 24, 1908 a concert by singer Lillian Nordich and the New York Symphony with Walter Damrosch merited utmost praise.

The Wilmington Orchestra gave several performances during the 1907-1908 season. A unique feature of the December concert was a composition by Alfred I. duPont. The beautiful gavotte pleased the audience immensely and evidently came up to the composer's requirements, as Mr. duPont smiled and bowed from the box. The March concert drew a large audience which voiced appreciation by liberal applause. Apparently the orchestra improved quickly and steadily. After the May concert, the *Every Evening* critic commented: "the growing favor of the orchestra is evidenced by the pleasure and appreciation of the audiences." A few minstrel groups, primarily Al Field and Lew Dockstaders, and a few opera companies performed each year.

Meeting Place

Gatherings which would attract large crowds were still held at the Opera House, although political rallies were often held at Turn Hall and at various meeting halls. A few days prior to election day 1904, citizens from all parts of the State gathered at the Opera House to listen to W. Bourke Cockran, the famous Democratic orator of New York. During the 1908 presidential campaign Judge Alton B. Parker, presidential candidate of 1904, addressed a capacity crowd at the Opera House. A parade of some 3,000 democratic clubmen, the largest parade of the campaign, marched down Market Street before the speech. The crowd gathered for Parker's speech was so large that an overflow meeting of some 2,000 people was held in the rear of the theatre and was addressed by F. Handy. The enthusiastic reception given to Parker was second only to the reception given to William Jennings Bryan, the candidate himself, when he appeared in Delaware on September 17. He spoke in Harrington, Delaware in the afternoon and in Wilmington in the evening. Because of the enormous turnout, conservatively estimated at 12,000 to 15,000, his Wilmington appearance was held outdoors at Shellpot Park. The closing meeting of the Democratic political campaign was held at the Opera House on October 31, 1908. A few days later, election returns were broadcast at the theatre.

Moving Pictures

The moving pictures which had begun so innocently began to assume more importance. In 1904 the Howe moving pictures were billed as events in their own right. During the 1905-1906 season, both the Howe and the Shepard moving pictures were presented. Then, in the summer of 1907, the Opera House broke with tradition and remained open during the summer months with a full program of moving pictures. The innovation was so successful that the management decided to continue the practice of showing films, a decision which influenced the fate of the theatre. In February 1908 the management inaugurated a moving picture series. As the *Every Evening* announced:

owing to the unprecedented success attained at the Grand Opera House last summer by the excellent quality of the moving pictures offered there, Resident Manager Johnson has decided to offer this unusually popular form of entertainment at this playhouse every afternoon and evening throughout the remainder of this season, when the house is not given over to the regular travelling organization or to local rentals.[4]

The films, which commenced that very afternoon, included: *The Merry Widow, Ben Hur, The Prodigal Son, The Great Trial, The Passion Play* and eight comedy pictures.

By the 1908-1909 season moving pictures were shown from October to March whenever there were no other attractions. On election night 1908, moving pictures and election returns were featured. Election returns came over telephone wires direct to the balcony of the theatre. Unfortunately, the ideal balance between live events and moving pictures could not be maintained, and only too soon moving pictures tipped the scales.

Vaudeville and the Bijou Circuit Company

Only a few major vaudeville companies appeared at the Opera House prior to 1909, yet vaudeville flourished at the Garrick, Avenue and Lyric theatres. However, in April 1909, the Bijou Circuit Company, which had sponsored many of the events brought to the Opera House, was given control of the theatre in order to experiment with a full vaudeville schedule. During April there were three

Market Street North from Eighth Street, 1915

vaudeville performances daily, composed of six acts and two reels of moving pictures. The vaudeville proved so successful that the Bijou Company wanted control of the house. During the summer a new lease was executed. After extensive renovations were completed by the new Bijou Company, the Opera House was opened in the fall as a first class, metropolitan vaudeville theatre. Three performances were held at 2:30, 7:30, and 9:00 daily; the entire show, which was exchanged with Bianey's Theatre in Baltimore, was changed on Monday and Thursday. During the incredible 1909-1910 season there were 200 days of vaudeville with three performances a day.

On August 30 the opening show included: Shean and Warren in *Quo Vadis Upside Down,* Marshall Montgomery ventriloquist and trick pianist, four dancing denos, Ali Hunter whirlwind dancers, the Taylor Twin Sisters Roller Skating Skit, and moving pictures. They all made a great hit: "Crowds began to gather in the lobby soon after dark and from that time until the second performance was well under way there was a rush for tickets."[5] On the second

day the *Every Evening* announced: "all records for business in Wilmington have been broken by the Opera House this week."

The acts which began on September 6 featured: the Peskoff Troupe of Russian Dancers, the Roger Trio of singing and dancing skits, John Zimmer juggler, Joe Lanigan monologist, the Sterlings lady and child talking act, motion pictures, and orchestra music. A total of 4,000 people paid admission to the three performances.

Despite the enormous success of vaudeville, in December 1909 the Bijou lease was transferred to the Harris Amusement Co. The new lessee continued the vaudeville attractions but lowered the prices to 10 cents for all performances. The Harris Company also advertised that once one paid admission one could stay as long as one liked—no need to leave at the end of the performance. The opening show on January 3 featured: a comedy playlet, *Jerry's Return;* the Gail Johnson Trio of Gymnasts; Tom Moan, Irish comedian; Kennedy and Kennedy, singing and dancing duos; and Ivy & Ivy, instrumentalists. The performances and the popular new prices were overwhelmingly successful, despite intense competition from the Garrick, two doors away; and a full program of vaudeville shows was continued until April 9. Two days after the vaudeville ceased, the Grand Inaugural of the Spring and Summer Season of moving picture shows was announced. Motion pictures were shown continually from 12 noon until 11 PM; admission was a minimal five cents; pictures changed every day. On April 14 the *Every Evening* reported the success of the series: "attendance yesterday broke all records and there is no doubt that the spring and summer season of moving pictures inaugurated by the Harris Amusement Co. will be a big success."

The Grand Error

Apparently the success of the summer series of moving pictures was too great; in September the Opera House continued to show moving pictures. Although the management announced that "it was probable but not certain that some theatrical attractions would be brought in during the season," only a bare minimum of live performances materialized. Instead of incorporating moving pictures—the current rage in entertainment—into their program, as it had done with changes in the past, the management suddenly substituted movies for the rich variety of live events. The resolution had dire consenquences. The Grand Opera House, which was built as a small, intimate house where people could share the warmth and excitement of a live performance, could not succeed as a first-rate movie theatre. The decision to convert the theatre into a movie house brought the Grand Era to its end.

SCENE SIX

THE CHANGING BUILDING

Just as the nature of the performances varied, the Masonic Hall itself changed continually between 1870 and 1910. Work included alterations to correct the original problems, adaptation to the times, as well as general maintenance and decorating matters.

Alterations

The perennial problem at the Opera House was the floor level and the sight line. During construction the Hall Co. feared that the stage line was high and asked Architect Dixon to reconsider its height. Mr. Dixon was firm in his statement that the hall was built according to the acoustical line which should govern in such matters. But from opening night on the sight line was a problem, as the *Every Evening* reported: "It is possible that the parquet is too low for the stage, but this can be easily remedied." [1]

Unfortunately the problem was not "so easily remedied." In May 1875 the Board met in the theatre to discuss the floor level. The janitor, *i.e.*, theatre manager, Mr. Baylis, blocked up several rows of seats to test a new level. Agreeing that the change was advantageous, the Board voted to raise the floor three inches at the stage and to preserve the same grade to the middle of the parquet circle, and then to raise the floor to the bottom of the first step or six inches. The changes, which were made in a few weeks, made the parquet chairs the best seats rather than the worst.

The 1875 correction turned out to be an improvement but not a solution. In 1886 the sight line was again a central issue when a Mr. Plouman of Philadelphia drew up plans for extensive renovations of the theatre. According to his plans the orchestra floor was to be raised back and sides to make it as large as the gallery front.

Mr. Plouman did not keep the terms of his contract; he did not furnish the necessary drawings to other contractors, and he failed to complete the work on schedule. Therefore the sight line might not have been altered exactly as his plans outlined. But by the fall the floor had been made level for about eight feet from the front of the stage, and the stage had been lowered.

During the summer of 1891, when control of the theatre returned to the Masonic Hall Co., the new manager, Mr. Williamson, recommended changing the floor level but no action was taken. In 1893, when Mr. Williamson again recommended raising the orchestra floor and raising benches on the side of the gallery, the Hall Co. did agree to change the auditorium floor between row T and the entrance door but elected not to make the gallery changes. In 1895 and 1898 changes were again discussed. As part of the extensive alterations made by the Bijou Circuit Company in 1909, a new floor was installed. The lower end of the floor near the orchestra was raised eight inches; the orchestra enclosure was left at its old level.[2]

Adaptations

The Opera House remained a viable theatre because it evolved with the times. The first major adaptation was the installation of electricity. The Masonic Hall Co. had experimented with electricity from the beginning of its existence in Wilmington. In 1883 the Armous Electric Co. of New Jersey opened its Wilmington operation by installing thirty-five arc lamps in the city.[3] In December one lamp was placed in the Opera House lobby for a tenant, the Provident Society. It was to be lit only on nights of performances for 60¢. The Company then began investigating the cost of installing electric lighting throughout the house. In April 1886 the Hall Co. decided *not* to use electricity because it would cost more than gas. A few months later the issue was being reconsidered when a Mr. W. C. Harris explained how electricity could be used to light gas. After careful deliberation, the committee decided that $248 to complete Mr. Harris' suggestions was "inexpedient at the present time." When the Hall Co. began encountering financial difficulty in 1887 it found even the cost of the one electric light too prohibitive and discontinued it. During the summer of 1888, when Proctor and Soulier leased the hall and promised to spend $5,000 in improvements, the company fully recognized the advantages of electricity and immediately installed it in the Opera House. The public was delighted with this major improvement. In the early fall, the *Every Evening* reported: "the house is lighted throughout with electricity and is as bright and as cozy as one could desire." [4]

In 1904 the building was changed in order to adapt to a stricter fire control. The city authorities informed the Hall Co. that they deemed it wise to consider measures to make egress from the theatre safer and surer in case of fire or panic. The required changes included: widening the lobby into the auditorium and removing several seats to make a wider entrance, making fire escapes from the gallery to the alley, and installing a water pipe and fire hose. Throughout the years the ground floor windows closest to Market Street had been used as extra fire exits into the alleys. Now two additional windows on each side of the auditorium were cut down to make even more exits. Further improvements included overhauling all of the electrical wires under the stage.

Another major adaptation to the times was the installation of an elevator in 1912. After debating the issue for nearly five years, all the Masonic bodies agreed to pay an increased rent in order to install the elevator. This made access to their third and fourth floor quarters much easier. In June 1912 Otis Elevator was contracted for $2,299.

Maintenance

By far the largest percentage of work fell into the general maintenance and decorating category. Work on the theatre was completed during the summer months when the theatre was closed because of the lack of cooling ventilation and the resulting common custom of outdoor excursions to the country. The amount of work varied from summer to summer depending on the condition of the building and the financial situation of the Company.

During the first ten years only a minimum of work was completed. The largest job was the alteration of the floor level in 1875. But the seats also showed deterioration. In 1879 Mr. Baylis was instructed to have the iron work of the chairs repainted. In June 1880 a few cast-iron pieces for the chairs were recast. During the summer of 1881 two dozen new chairs were cast. Evidently the materials began to show signs of decay and, in 1880, the front railing of the balcony was changed from upholstery to wood coping for $60. The next summer the coping around the boxes and orchestra circle was changed to walnut trimmings. New matting was installed in the entry, and the carpet was cleaned.

However in 1882, ten years after the opening of the theatre, extensive improvements were made. After ten years with relatively little work, the theatre was in poor condition. Furthermore, the Hall Co. had the funds to refurbish the house since the receipts from the 1881-1882 season were the highest of any previous season—income from the theatre and the lecture hall was $10,549.19. The theatre was painted and papered. In July the Hall Co. received proposals for papering the walls of the auditorium. Each proposal agreed to wash off the fresco on the walls, size the walls, and use fifty gilt paper with a nine-inch frieze on top and bottom. Mr. S. N. Anderson, the low bidder, was awarded the contract for $130. The hall was painted by Cardwall and Wall, a local company. The proscenium front was repainted in oil and water for twenty dollars by L. H. Quay, a well respected local painter, who also frescoed the Masonic blue room. All of the seats in the orchestra circle were reupholstered by Granville Worrell for $625. According to the *Every Evening* the seats were upholstered in raw silk.

Only three years later, in 1885, painting and papering were again necessary. Cardwall and Wall were contracted to paint for $390. The lobby was papered by Joseph Greenman for $162.

In 1886 Mr. Plouman of Philadelphia was hired for $4,000 to make extensive changes in the theatre. The incentive was simple— the new Academy of Music had opened in January 1886. A few weeks before the Academy opened, the Masonic Hall Co.'s decision to renovate and improve the Opera House so that it would compare favorably with the new Academy of Music was reported in the *Every Evening*. But the Academy of Music created such a sensation at its January opening that some improvements were made to the Opera House even sooner—in February. On February 11, the *Every Evening* reported that the Opera House was "conspicuously clean and bright Wednesday evening."

But the majority of work was done during the summer of 1886 under the direction of Mr. Plouman. The plans called not only for a change in the floor level but for new seats. A. H. Andrews and Co. of New York was awarded the contract for new chairs: 354 in the orchestra at $4.50 each and 498 in the orchestra circle for $3.00 each—total cost $3,263.40. Mr. Plouman was negligent in producing new floor drawings for the seating company, and the work was thrown behind schedule. The Hall Co. had to change the September 11 opening and had to pay an additional 10% so that some seats would be available on September 13. The installation of new parquet seats was not complete until 5 o'clock on opening day, September 13. The old orchestra chairs had to be temporarily set up because of the delay in the arrival of the new ones. According to the *Every Evening,* the seating capacity was about the same as before. The gallery seats, which were repaired by Hodges for 28½ cents each, were reupholstered by Granville Worrell for a total of $171.05.

Other work done during the summer of 1886 included painting and gilting by L. H. Quay, refrescoing the proscenium by N. Goldberg, and repairs to the heating apparatus, the stage area, and scenery.

Despite the extent of these repairs, the theatre was apparently in poor condition. Less than two years later, when Proctor and Soulier assumed management of the theatre, the company declared the theatre in need of major improvements and promised to invest $5,000 on improvements before September 1 and $1,000 per year for each succeeding year. During the first summer, the summer of 1888, the installation of electricity was a major expense. The lobby was also altered considerably according to plans presented in June. The ticket box office was to be brought out twenty feet. Despite some Masonic opposition, the changes were made. It is probable that a second box office for the gallery was installed on the second floor at this time, since in the fall there were complaints about the box office noise on the second floor for the first time. When Proctor and Soulier signed the contract in January 1888 they promised to raise the proscenium arch, remove the partition at the rear of the house, substitute glass windows, and change the location of boxes nearest the proscenium. No later mention is made of these changes, so it is not certain if they were completed. However, the new appearance of the house was greatly praised by the *Every Evening* which described the theatre as:

... brilliantly illuminated with electric lamps and the effects wrought thru work of renovation were seen to excellent advantage. Aside from numerous improvements to the gallery and lobby, the most striking feature is the bright and cheerful aspect of the house through frescoing ... the walls are in rich tints brought out through dashes of warm coloring. The lobby has been paved in tiles, redecorated and handsomely frescoed. The stage and scenery are greatly improved. Through the ingenious electrical apparatus, the most artistic effects are produced on stage.[5]

As part of their commitment to expend $1,000 per year on improvements, in 1889, Proctor and Soulier corrected a major sound problem. The sound of the curtain was bothering the Masons in their lodge rooms so heavy paper was put on the ceiling under the lodge rooms to keep noise from ascending. During the summer of 1890 Proctor and Soulier were very discontent and were trying to rid themselves of the Opera House. The only change recorded is the repair of the lumber grids over the stage.

By the summer of 1891 control had reverted to the Masonic Hall Co. with Mr. Williamson as manager. Under his direction, the stage area was the scene of extensive improvements. The false proscenium, which so often caused awkward moments to retiring actors, was removed. Movable doorways were substituted. The change afforded an additional five feet of stage on either side. Furthermore, the boxes on either side of the stage were cut down to allow those seated at the sides a better view of the stage. Underneath the stage everything was new. Two new dressing rooms were bulit and the others were repainted. The star dressing room was moved to the left of the stage. The floor underneath the stage which had rotted away was relaid. The balcony and stairway were matted. New scenery was purchased. In the hall itself, the ceiling beneath the balcony was painted in light blue. According to the *Every Evening*, the "new tone painting was the greatest relief from the dingy tone hitherto existing. It is painted in blue and sheds a pleasant brightness all around." As the *Every Evening* reported, the public was well pleased with the changes: "upon entering the auditorium, the visitor is impressed with a very gratifying sensation of comfort and pleasure at the improvements observable all around." [6] During the summer of 1892, changes were made because the electric light was deficient.

In 1893 the appearance of the house was again replenished for a familiar incentive, the Academy of Music was reopening with the new name of People's Theatre. The floor level downstairs was changed during 1893. Although the idea of raising the benches on the side of the gallery was not approved, the balcony was improved with the installation of eighty new chairs, each costing $1.50. The rigging on the stage was improved by building a fly gallery. The walls of one side under the gallery were washed off and repaired. On opening night, the *Every Evening* called the theatre "one of the handsomest amusement houses in the country."

Although there were no major alterations during the summer of 1894, two visible changes did take place in the stage area. A drop curtain with advertisements was painted by the Scenic Ad Co. of Philadelphia. The Hall Co. promised to use the curtain between every act of every performance for at least five minutes. The Scenic Co. guaranteed the curtain would be of a highly artistic order, interesting, realistic, and in harmony with the interior decorations. Repairs were also made into the dressing rooms.

For nearly ten years no major decorating is described. In 1898 a new floor was laid on the stage, and the hallway was repapered. In 1899 the plastering over the stage front was repaired, and the frescoing around the proscenium was renewed. Then, after nearly 10 years, in 1902 the interior of the auditorium was painted for $213 by Keenan and Brothers. The hallway was painted and brightened. Gallery chairs were overhauled and recovered for $70 by E. L. Peacock and Co.

In the spring of 1903 the auditorium committee was instructed to look over the interior of the theatre to make suggestions for replenishing and decorating. The hall was repainted, a new carpet was installed in the aisles, and a new pendant was hung from the ceiling.

By 1907 the concerns were with the structure. A cement floor was installed in the lobby of the auditorium. The stairs between the first and second floors were repaired.

During the summer of 1909 the theatre was completely transformed into a thoroughly up-to-date metropolitan theatre. The entire interior was ripped out; everything was made new and modern, in order to make the house more comfortable for patrons and more convenient for players.[7]

After the new floor was installed the seating pattern was complete rearranged. The center aisle was eliminated; all the seats would now run in lines north and south across the house. There were eight boxes on the main floor level. The gallery was divided into a balcony and gallery. Since the lower section of the balcony was considered an excellent place from which to see and hear, it was furnished as comfortably as the main floor. The seating capacity of the entire theatre was 1,552, or 300 more than in the original house. The heats were all new "of the latest approved pattern with ball bearings." The chairs on the lower floor were upholstered in green leather; the balcony chairs were not upholstered. The walls were painted light and dark green and were trimmed in gold. The dressing rooms and facilities beneath the stage were completely remodeled. The Bijou Circuit Co. had spent some $17,000 and had converted the Opera House into a first-rate vaudeville house, which would compete with the Garrick.

Designing a new façade was discussed, but the company decided to wait and satisfied itself by installing a large electric sign, which was ironically considered an innovation, over the entrance.

Actually very little had been done to the façade since 1871. It was repainted periodically in 1878, 1881, 1894, and 1904. No major work was undertaken until the turn of the century when the entrance way was widened and bulk windows, which provided additional display space, were installed. In 1901 Mr. Alfred Downward was contracted to complete these changes for $4,458.

The roof of the Masonic Hall presented continual problems. As early as November 1872, less than a year after the opening, the Masonic building committee reported that the roof of the front of the building seemed to be "settling under the towers." The girders should be strengthened before the snow." The girders were strengthened and all was well until September 1876, when a severe snow storm unroofed most of the auditorium and damaged the main roof. The roof was covered with two thicknesses of roof felting to prevent any damage from rain. Two years later, after inspecting the roof, the Engineer of Bridges, E. K. Larkin, declared it unsafe and demanded that rods be installed to make the roof safe again. Although this work was completed in the summer, a new roof was contracted in the fall. The safety of the roof was discussed again in 1881. Roof repairs were made in 1886, 1891, 1893, and 1903. Furthermore, the roof was repainted every few years.

Scenery

One of the most frequent areas of maintenance, not part of the hall itself but of prime importance to the function of the theatre, was the scenery.

Russell Smith had equipped the Opera House with a full set of fine scenery. As early as September 1873 the Masonic Hall Co. decided it needed more scenes and ordered a library scene from Mr. Smith for $175. In November a stone wall, as well as a court room scene with the judges' stand and the prisoners' box, was added to the stock. With these additional pieces the scenery served well until the 1880s, when repairs began to occur with great frequency. The poor condition might be attributed to the lack of care taken by travelling troupes. During the summer of 1880 William Schaeffer, a scenic artist, was paid $140.87 to paint two new scenes and to touch up the old ones. Although no repairs were made during the next two seasons, the stage setting was enhanced with a new suit of furniture purchased for $85 in November 1883.

In June 1884 the Company decided it would be unwise to purchase any new secenry, but it hired a Mr. Hawthorn to change and repaint some of the old scenes. Mr. Hawthorn worked so slowly that the committee feared the scenery would not be finished by the opening, so a second man was hired at $35 per week. By the fall, six new scenes were complete and work on the horizon and wood wings continued.

As part of the extensive repairs of 1886 Mr. Farron of Philadelphia was hired at $30 per week to repair the scenery. Mr. Farron worked throughout the major part of August. In 1887 Mr. R. P. Fraim painted a new parlor garden scene. During the improvements of 1888 Proctor and Soulier was granted the use of the stage when not in use for painting scenery. In 1891 Mr. J. B. Ayers painted more scenery. In 1892 $375 was authorized for alterations to the stage and scenery. The scene painted was paid $198.20 for his work. Additional repairs were made in 1894 and 1904.

As a result of continual changes, the Opera House of 1910 was very different from the Opera House of 1871. Although some alterations improved the quality of the house and others only satisfied someone's decorating preferences, all the changes maintained the theatre in first-rate condition. But with the end of the Grand Era, everything changed. Deterioration loomed in the wings.

INTERMISSION
THE TENANTS

814

Howe Sewing Machine Co.
1872-1877
Merrick & Drake, Auctioneers
1877-1880
Domestic Sewing Machine Co.
1883-1893
Singer Sewing Machine
1894-1895
Bradfield Pianos
1896-1898
VACANT
U.S. Express Office
1904-1915

816

Grover & Baker, Sewing Machine Co.
1872-1874
Sublet to George Macan
Pancoast Allen
1876-1886
George Drake, Autioneer
1889-1891
Dr. Hœgelsburger
1892-1899
Lawton Optical Co.
1899-1903
S. Luther McKee, Optician
1904-1928

820-822

Granville Worrell
1872-1888
Saul Speakman
1888-1892
J. Ford Fox
1896-1897
Dearborn Piano Co.
1898-1899
VACANT

820

Goodley & Sons
1902-1916

822

Hart & Colburns
1902-1903
John Porter Co.
1904
W. C. Hunt Co.
1905
Thomas Lawson
1906-1935

The Masonic Temple was more than an architectural masterpiece and a fine performing arts center. Because of its prime location, it was also an important commercial center. Numerous tenants, who prospered in the Masonic Hall during the Grand era, not only added character to the center but also provided an essential source of income. From the outset the Masons had the foresight to include commercial space in their new temple. Dixon's earliest preliminary sketches of June 1869 include "two large stores" on the ground level as well as rental space on the upper stories. Recognizing the importance of tenants, the Masons appointed a committee to consider renting the "cellar, stores and offices in the main building" six months before the interior of the theatre was finished.

The First Tenants

By working day and night during December the builders managed to complete the theatre by December 21, 1871; the commercial space was not available until several months later. The first tenant to enter the new building was the Board of Trade, an organization that had been formed in 1868 for the "mutual counsel and deliberation on business interests, manufacturing, commerce and trade of the city."[1] They moved into the front rooms on the second floor from their old premises on Third and Market Streets towards the end of March 1872. This organization provided $400 rent a year and, as a prestigious group, established an air of dignity to being an Opera House tenant. Mr. T. A. E. Rossitter, a clerk, also occupied his office space in late March. The Masonic bodies themselves rented a large portion of the upper floors from the Masonic Hall Co. The Joint Committee of Lodges agreed in November 1871 to rent the Mansard roof story for twenty years as well as some rooms over the auditorium on the third floor.

April 18, 1872 was the grand day of the Masonic order's formal entrace into the new temple. Led by the Grand Marshal, the subordinate lodges marched from Third and King Streets to the new temple where a ritualistic ceremony by the Architect and the Grand Marshal took place. The national aires of England, Germany, France, and the United States were sung in order to emphasize the universality of Masonry. An elaborate feast completed the celebration.

The Historical Society of Delaware also moved into their new premises on the third floor (lower side front and back) in April 1872. In the fall the additional office space was rented by: the Mendelssohn Club, Mrs. Pusey and Mr. Williamson, Howard Pyle, and one very important long-term tenant, Dr. Murphy—the principal of the Rugby Academy—a Select English, Classical, and Commercial Institution which became one of Wilmington's leading schools. The early tenants in the upper stories were representative of the type of tenants who paraded in and out of the temple during the ensuing years. Some, like the Board of Trade, stayed only a few years; others remained for more than a decade.

The prime real estate of four stores on the ground level were not occupied until nearly autumn. Grover, Baker Sewing Machine Company rented store 816 in late August for $750 per year. In December Howe Sewing Machine Co. leased store 814 for $800 per year.

In the fall Mr. Granville Worrell, a dry goods retailer, rented the two northern stores, 820 and 822. Mr. Worrell, who modeled himself after John Wanamaker, opened a dry goods store which featured silks, shawls, and dress materials. Ironically, he rented a space which Mr. Wanamaker might have leased. While searching for tenants the rental committee had contracted Mr. John Wanamaker in Philadelphia. In March they received a polite refusal:

Accept thanks for your esteemed favor and kind suggestions and thought to opening seems to be a very excellent one—we are so much occupied with our business here we fear we could not do justice to a new establishment in your beautiful town.

By renting 820 and 822 as one store Mr. Worrell established a trend. The store continued to be rented as one unit until nearly the turn of the century.

By December all the rental space in the building was occupied and the Masonic order could boast of the successful establishment of a god source of income. The stores provided close to $3,000 income. The tenants in the upper rooms paid close to $2,500; $1,400 from Masonic bodies, $400 from the Board of Trade, approximately $100 from Murphy and eight other small tenants.

1873-1910

Tenants varied with the times. Sometimes there were vacancies, but generally the commercial areas were a fine source of income. In

December 1883, the annual fiscal report listed $4,374 from the rental of rooms and stores; in 1889, $11,784; in 1910, $6,722.

The four ground floor stores attracted numerous businesses which are outlined in the accompanying chart. Although there were some vacancies, usually because the rent was too high, the stores were basically occupied.

The severest decline in rentals occurred at the turn of the century when, for a few years, only 814 was rented. But the public-spirited Masons permitted others to benefit from their misfortune and allowed local groups to use the vacant store on a temporary basis. For instance, the Elks used the store in 1900 while preparing for a street carnival. The Masonic Hall Company often granted rent reductions as well as some financial aid for physical improvements like papering and heating.

Similar stores were often attracted to the premises; competitors often occupied the premises at the same time. Sewing machine companies, music companies, and opticians were·the most reoccurring tenants.

Mr. Granville Worrell, the dry goods retailer who occupied 820 and 822 from 1872 to 1888, continually expanded his store. The business depression of 1875 affected Mr. Worrell so adversely that he had to request a reduction in rent, but by autumn 1876 business had improved and Mr. Worrell requested permission to rent the basements of stores 814 and 816. The Masonic Hall Co. declined to rent the basements because it might interfere with the rental of those stores. During the 1880s, Mr. Worrell continued to expand the inventory of his store, which sold dry goods, carpets, and upholstery, but by 1884 he complained that since business in this place had not been what it should have been, he must request a reduction in rent of $300 per year. He cited the location as his reason for a rent reduction: ". . . the increased cost over any other place in insurance . . . the proximity of the Opera House and the dancing room over us which attracts a crowd of people of such a kind that it is a continual detriment to our trade." Mr. Worrell also stated that he did not want to leave if it was possible to remain. The Masons obliged him by granting $200 for refurbishing his store and by agreeing to a reduced rent.

By the spring of 1885 Mr. Worrell's operation was a major portion of the Opera House. His expanded inventory covered several rooms: Street Floor—tapestry, engrain damask; Basement 1—under the above—upholstery goods; Basement 2—next to basement 1—oil cloths, cocoa matting; Basement 3—next to other—finer carpets.[2] In January 1886 Mr. Worrell rented the lecture room for a three year period and built a direct stairway from his store to the lecture room. Apparently Mr. Worrell expanded too quickly because by 1887 he was having trouble paying his rent on time. After continual warnings, the Masonic Hall Co. had to proceed legally against Mr. Worrell, and by the end of 1888 he was forced to vacate. Mr. Worrell briefly continued his carpet and upholstery business at 501 Shipley Street until financial difficulties forced him to end business.

Combined stores 820-822 were rented to Mr. Saul Speakman, proprietor of an installment house which specialized in furniture, carpets, window shades, and served as agents for the new Home Sewing Machine. Mr. Speakman's store only remained for four or five years.

Sewing machine companies had an affinity to the Opera House. Both 814 and 816 were originally rented to sewing machine companies. The Howe Sewing Machine Co. remained in 814 for some five years. The space was rented briefly by William Merrick and George Drake, auctioneers, but by 1884, the space was rented by the Domestic Sewing Machine Company, manufacturers of machines, paper fashions, as well as dealers in needles, oil, and attachments of all kinds for sewing machines. The Domestic Company, an eight-year tenant, still occupied 814 when Mr. Speakman in 820-822 was the agent for Home Sewing Machines. Early in 1891 the Domestic Sewing Machine Company requested the passage from the rear of their store to the water closet enclosed from the rain and storms for the convenience of their clients. Although the required work was done, by 1893 the Domestic Sewing Machine Company vacated their premises. After the store was vacant for two years the Singer Sewing Machine Company, the third sewing machine company to occupy 814, rented the space for two years.

Grover and Baker, the first tenants in 816, only remained in their premises for two year at which time they sublet to George Macan, an upholsterer who had been contracted for work on the theatre hall during 1871. In 1875 when the space was being rented, all the applicants claimed the rent ($800 including heat) was too high. Finally in 1876 the store was rented to Pancoast Allen for $450.

Pancoast Allen and his original partner, Freeborne Smith, were music dealers. This store, specilaizing in pianos and organs, remained until February 1887, at which time the effects in the store were seized for failure to pay the rent. After Mr. Allen was removed, he became a music teacher. The store was briefly rented to auctioneer George Drake, who had formerly rented 814. In 1889 Grant S. Riggs rented the space for a shop specializing in "gent's furnishing and fine neckware."

Music shops were another Masonic Temple "regular." Pancoast Allen's shop occupied 816 for ten years. In 1896 Mr. John Ford Fox opened a piano and organ shop in 820-822; in the same year Bradfield Pianos, who specialized in pianos, organs, and all musical instruments, moved into 814. After one year Mr. Fox transferred his lease to the Dearborn Piano Company which stocked the latest styles of pianos and organs. In 1899 the Dearborn Company renewed the lease only on store 822, thereby ending the nearly thirty years of joint rental.

Optometry entered the Masonic Temple with Dr. Hoegelsberger who rented 816 from 1892 to 1899. After Dr. Hoegelsberger vacated, the Lawton Optical Company rented the shop from 1899 to 1903. When the Lawton Optical Co. vacated, S. Luther McKee took the lease until 1928. At the turn of the century, incidently, the Lawton Optical Co. was the only occupied store.

Over the years the Masonic idea of suitable tenants changed. In 1872 when Mr. Worrell requested permission to use the basement of his shop for a billiard saloon, he was categorically denied permission. But in the late 1880s, when Mr. Joseph B. Harding requested the basement of the southside for a billiard room, the Masons agreed to study the propriety of it. In February 1888 the basement was rented to him for $400. The saloon, which turned into a very successful amusement center, remained in the building until 1910.

During a forty-year period the tenants in the upper stories varied continually. Although the Masonic lodges shifted spaces around, they always reserved a large portion of the upper stories for themselves. Several individuals and small businesses rented office space, but the majority of tenants in the upper floors were the local clubs. The H.Y.M.A. Society, the Beethoven Club, the Dramatic Association, the Adonis Club, Neptune Club, Oriole Club, and Philharmonic Association were among more than 50 groups which occupied the rooms for varying degrees of time. Several Masonic groups, *e.g.,* St. Johns Commandery and Knights Templar, were tenants.

Two of the upper floor tenants merit special attention because of the character they added to the building during the 1880s: Webster's Dancing Academy and the Rugby Academy. In 1876 Ayres S. Webster was a machinist by profession who ran a private dancing academy at the Masonic Temple as a sideline. Although he did not rent any permanent space at this time, he did use space in the building for his private lessons which were given at the convenience of the client. By 1878 Mr. Webster, now a dancing teacher, held numerous classes in his quarters as well as special events in the main theatre. At least twelve balls were held in Mr. Webster's room during the 1878-1880 seasons. Among the very successful functions were balls by the Orion Club, Knights of Pithias, H.Y.M.A., Washington Assembly, Gnaker Assembly, and the Montefiore Society. The ball of Montefiore Society in February 1880 was typical of the "high style" of the balls. Well before the ball began the rooms were crowded with ladies and gentlemen from Philadelphia, Chester, West Chester, and Dover. A seven-piece orchestra, under the direction of Mr. Ritchie, furnished the music which began with a grand march at 9:30 P.M. Refreshments were served at midnight in the lecture-banquet room; then dancing continued until early morning. The ball, which was held to raise funds for the erection of a synagogue and employment of a Hebrew teacher, was so successful that the Montefiore Society held annual balls in Webster's rooms. Obviously Mr. Webster's quarters were not too large. When a ball of the Weccacoe Actives attracted 150 couples, the scene was described as chaotic and disorderly. By the early 1880s Mr. Webster's academy was so successful that he moved to greatly expanded quarters on the fourth floor. But times changed. When Webster's was declined a rent reduction in 1889, he vacated the premises.

The Rugby Academy, founded in 1872, became the principal boy's school in Wilmington by 1876. Instruction was offered in ancient languages, French language and literature, German language and literature, history, natural sciences, mathematics, bookkeeping, freehand drawing and mechanical drawing, and penmanship.[3] In 1872 the headmaster, Dr. Murphy, rented the available rooms on the second floor; however, as tenants vacated their premises, the school expanded. By 1876 the Rugby Academy occupied most of the second floor—four large rooms. One room contained about fifty desks of the juniors and seniors; a second room held some twenty odd desks for the primary school; a third room was used for recitations; and the fourth room was a gymnasium.[4] The school, which remained in the Opera House until 1887, also included boarding facilities in Wilmington's outstanding hotel, the Clayton House.

The Rugby Literary Society, the senior's club for recitations, essays, and debates, held their annual exhibition which was a major social event for youngsters in the Opera House. The school's graduation was always held in the theatre. Another benefit to the location was that military drills were held in Webster's premises on the top floor. The Academy was a short-lived success. By the end of the 1880s its reputation declined, the school left the Opera House, and was closed.

More than eighty different tenants occupied the Masonic Temple between 1870 and 1910. Not only did their presence provide income essential to operating the building; it also added a new dimension to the city and the hall. Characterizing the building as an "ambitious move that would result in the general benefit to social enjoyment and trade of the city," the *Every Evening* appealed to the "business duty of society and business men" to support the new endeavor. The new hall furnished commercial and meeting space at an important location in the expanding city. Undoubtedly some citizens, uninterested in theatre, knew the Masonic Hall only as a shopping center and meeting place. By expanding the number of people who used the hall and the range of services offered by the building, the tenants increased the vitality of the building. The Masonic Hall, with its temple, theatre, commercial, and meeting space, played a significant rôle in the social history of 19th century Delaware.

ACT 3

❦

FALL FROM GRANDEUR

1911-1970

Parade on Market Street, 1914

Moving pictures were fatal to the Opera House. After September, 1910, the Opera House was primarily a movie theatre, although some live performances were mixed with the moving pitcures during the early years, 1910-1913. In 1911 Al C. Fields and his big minstrel company were advertised as "the banner attraction" at this popular playhouse. Before the performance on January 16 the troupe marched through the streets and attracted a huge crowd which filled the house to capacity at both performances. The Philadelphia Orchestra continued to play its annual Wilmington series at the Opera House. The 1910-1911 series "wound up with a blaze of orchestral fireworks in the shape of a great Wagner night on February 20." [1] Conductor Carl Pohlig was considered one of the greatest Wagnerian interpreters; operatic soloist Anna Case was superb. The successful 1912-1913 season was held under the direction of Leopold Stokowski, the orchestra's new conductor who was described as: "a musician very young and very wonderful ... (who) had taken Philadelphia by storm and won them by his magnetism, poise and self mastery."[2] After the opening concert on November 11, 1912 the local critic announced "last night he conquered Wilmington." The Philadelphia orchestra concerts were so important that, as a phase of cultural training, young men in the orchestra of Wilmington High School received free tickets to the concerts. One giant step downwards was taken in the fall of 1913 when the Philadelphia orchestra transferred its series to the Playhouse, which had been built in the Hotel duPont during the summer.

Stripped of its musical tradition, the Opera House became primarily a movie theatre. The Garrick and the Avenue (later called Empire) were the chief vaudeville housese in town. The Playhouse began attracting the outstanding stars of the day who had formerly graced the Opera House. After a few months, a local critic praised the Playhouse for providing the stimulus for increased dramatic events: . . . a new and keen interest in things dramatic which had lain dormant for want of nourishment has sprung into being with the opening of the new playhouse.[3]

The Harris Amusement Co.'s concept of lowering the admission price to five cents had long range implications. The theatre became known for serials and continuous shows, not for first-run movies.

During the teens and twenties one could enter the theatre for five cents and stay all day. Children flocked to the theatre on Saturdays for a full afternoon of entertainment. Piano music always accompanied the programs of full-length films and serials. *The Perils of Pauline, Marnie,* and *Dr. Jekyll and Mr. Hyde* were some of the popular attractions of those years.

Meanwhile the great moving pictures of the day, often made by stars who had formerly appeared at the Opera House, were shown at the Majestic, the Queen, and the Arcadia. For instance, the film version of *The Count of Monte Cristo,* starring James O'Neill, appeared at the Majestic in 1913. Maurice Chevalier in *The Big Pond* was shown at the Arcadia. Frank Mayo in *Hitching Posts* was shown at the Rialto. John Barrymore's famous film *The Man from Blankley* premiered at the Queen.

But since the Harris Amusement Co., managed by Senator John Harris of Pennsylvania, had exclusive rights to the Fox pictures, with their advanced sound system called movietone, 20th Century Fox films were also shown at the Opera House. Obviously the theatre

135

was successful because in the late 1920s the Harris Amusement Co. attempted to negotiate a thirty-year lease with the Masonic Hall Co. The Masons were not interested in such a long term lease.

In June 1930 the lease was assumed by Warner Brothers who already owned several theatres in downtown Wilmington: the Aldine, Arcadia, Savoy, and Queen. Since Warner Brothers already had four top houses for grade A and good grade B films, they did not need the Grand, an older theatre, for top run films. Instead, Warner Brothers converted the Grand into a theatre for western and action films—films that could not stand up by themselves as first run movies. Buck Jones in *The Ivory Handled Gun,* Victor Jones in *Escape from Devil's Island,* Helen Twelvetrees in *The Spanish Cape Mystery,* and Hopalong Cassidy were typical of the popular westerns and mysteries shown at the Grand.

136

The Saturday matinées were a great favorite. On Saturday, February 17, 1940 the offerings, typical of the matinées, included: the feature western *Roaming Wild* and two serials, the last chapter of *The Phantom Creeps,* and the first chapter of *The Green Hornet.*

Sometimes first run westerns were featured: in January 1940 the new Roy Rogers film, *Saga of Death Valley;* in 1945 *One Body Too Many* and *When Strangers Marry.* Buster Crabtree, Laurel & Hardy, Gene Autry, Ken Mayward, Ellery Queen, and Boston Blackie were some of the more popular names in this era. But increasingly during the Warner years the theatre became known as a "sluff house," a theatre for films which were not strong enough for first runs.

By the 1960s the caliber of the films had declined still further; films were "received off the drive-ins and their showing at the Grand was the last run in Wilmington." Inferior westerns and horror films were presented as double features. When the Grand theatre, as it was known in those years, made the news, the problem was often violence. A false fire alarm was sent out in 1952; the box office attendant was held up in 1958. Police had to rush to the theatre to calm a disturbance of several youths climbing on the stage and dancing in 1965. Children in the audience were often hit by candy bombs. But one tradition, reminiscent of the "grand days" survived—an annual free Christmas party for children was given by the Red Star Wallpaper & Paint Co.

Physical Decline

As the role of the building changed, its appearance was altered dramatically and symbolically. The façade, which had not undergone major changes during the Grand years, was completely transformed during the 20th century.

The first change was the addition of the neon Grand sign which the Bijou Co. installed in 1909. It was considered a great modern improvement. In 1911 the Hall Co. gave the Harris Amusement Co. authorization to sell the awning over the entrance. The entrance was defaced when the Harris Co. built the huge marquise over the main entrance in 1921.

A fire destroyed the roof, the fourth floor façade, and the banquet room in the fall of 1934. By early December the necessary re-

Renovation of the interior, 1943

pairs had been made at an estimated $23,300, but the repairs merely included protection—no elaborate architectural features were restored. The three cupolas were not rebuilt; the decorative iron grillwork was not replaced.

As the stores deteriorated and needed repairs modern storefronts which completely hid the elegant cast-iron of the ground level were installed.

By 1940, the exterior of the Grand Opera House was completely defaced—ironically in the name of progress. The Grand began to look like a second rate movie theatre—the image of the elegant Opera House had vanished.

The interior followed a similar pattern. In 1913 a movie booth was built; in 1925 it was expanded and blocked the major entrance to the balcony. A huge movie screen permanently attached to the stage became the dominant stage attraction. The entire theatre was repainted in dull green and later covered in padding and satin in order to "improve acoustics" for moving pictures.

The final blow occurred in 1943 when, for structural reasons, it was necessary to install large steel trusses beneath the Masonic rooms on the third floor. A flat ceiling was built below the trusses for fire protection. By this the frescoed ceiling, the "crowning glory," was also hidden. In spite of its changed appearance and rôle, the Grand did continue to function.

Throughout the century the population of the city had shifted. Between 1920-1960 the city population decreased by about 14,000, while the population in the suburban areas around the city increased from 38,000 to 211,000. The city became a place where there was more substandard housing, fewer college graduates, fewer professional workers, and fewer skilled laborers. Violence and racial tension grew.

Due to the decline in the city, business at city theatres suffered. The Stanley Warner Corporation began dissolving many theatres in Delaware in order to build new ones in suburban areas of New Jersey and Pennsylvania. In 1967 the Warner Corporation decided not to renew its lease on the Grand. No one else wanted to lease it, either. On June 30, after the Grand's double feature, *Hotel* and *The Game is Over,* the audience left, the lights went out, and the Grand theatre was dark.

The days of Grand entertainment were gone.

ACT 4

v

RETURN TO GRANDEUR
1971-1976

SCENE ONE

SELECTION OF THE SITE

As the curtain rises in April 1968 the Grand Opera House stands deformed and abandoned in the midst of a city which has become a cultural and civic wasteland. Racial tension, which continued to grow in the 1960s, has just reached an extreme after the assassination of Dr. Martin Luther King. The recent efforts to revitalize the Grand Theatre are dead. Only the Wilmington Playhouse, tucked away safely in the Hotel duPont, continues to bring theatrical performances to the downtown area.

The revitalization effort which climaxed in the fall of 1967 had its roots back in the mid-sixties. As part of the general Downtown Plan developed by the city and Greater Wilmington Development Council in 1965-1967, GWDC considered building a Civic Center which would include a convention hall and auditorium at 4th and King Streets. For a time, there seemed to be a possibility of including an art center within the project. Therefore, in 1966, as an adjunct to the GWDC effort, a citizens' group chaired by local architect William Pelham began meeting to discuss the needs of the artistic community. Members of the group all agreed that the arts needed a new shelter; that there was no place for people to congregate in the city. The arts in Delaware would be stimulated if fine artists had a better place to exhibit and performing artists had a better place to perform.

For more than a year and a half the committee of concerned citizens continued to meet. When the new GWDC center no longer seemed a viable possibility for the arts, the committee began looking for more immediate means and studied the Sayer Building on 18th and Market Streets. The possibilities of adapting this fine buliding to artistic purposes seemed excellent, but in the final analysis proved too expensive.

By 1967 the Wilmington Opera Society, faced with price and scheduling problems at the Playhouse, began to investigate the possibility of renting the Grand Theatre from the Masons. Preliminary studies of the building led the society's leaders to conclude that the Grand Theatre could be converted into a house suitable for any one of the arts and that such a facility was needed by the community. According to President Eric Kjellmark the Opera Society's intention was to "rent the hall from the Masons and to do just enough clean up work to allow the Opera Society and other local organizations to use the building."[1]

Restoration to this point, including stage renovation, lighting, seating, dressing rooms, and heating, would require $50,000 to $75,000 of capital improvements.[2] As the potential of the building became clear, Kjellmark and others began meeting with community leaders interested in the arts and contacted Mr. Pelham, President of the Cultural Affairs Center Committee. During the summer the Opera Society hired Mr. Pelham to conduct a preliminary investigation of the building. After consulting acoustical, structural, lighting, heating, fire and safety, and backstage experts, Mr. Pelham presented a new cost estimate of $954,000 to renovate the theatre and backstage areas.[3] The study, which was quite preliminary, did not even include removing the false storefronts. Clearly, the intent at this point was a renovation not a major restoration.

During the summer the Opera Society decided the project was too large for it to handle alone, so it handed the project over to a special building committee with Joe Angell as chairman. Local newspapers promoted the project. Local reporter Bill Frank claimed: "to destroy it would be a crime; to restore it would be a triumph."[4] In August 1967, when critic-at-large Otto Dekom emphasized the need for a center, an editorial stated:

whatever is done, the Grand certainly is deserving of consideration for restoration, and as Mr. Dekom urges let's dream no small dreams in seeking the theatre's preservation.

Despite growing enthusiasm for the project, it did not go much further. As Mr. Angell explains, "it was simply too big at that time and enough community support could not be mustered." Silence returned to the Grand.

For nearly two years the theatre was vacant. Even the Masons renewed their discussion about leaving the hall and building a new one in the suburbs. In 1969 the theatre was temporarily rescued by Mr. Chuck Powell who rented the theatre to show action films: westerns, adventures, gangster, and occasional horror films—at reasonable prices. Mr. Powell emphasized that the public needed and wanted action films. The theatre would appeal to all ages but would charge only 50¢ admission for children.

Despite the theatre being open, restoration enthusiasts would not let the "grand idea" die. Journalists kept the idea alive. Bill Frank, Emerson Wilson, and others continued to retell moments of the Grand's history in order to engender enthusiasm. Bill Pelham and Joe Angell continued to discuss the Grand Theatre, ecpecially around the GWDC office, where both were involved in studies of the Sayer Building. In the spring of 1971 Mr. Pelham addressed the first meeting of the Victorian Society in American and spoke on the Opera House as the finest piece of Victorian architecture in the city.

But nothing was happening. As Bill Frank had incitefully stated, "the problem of the restoration resorted to the usual Wilmington question, "Who's going to do all this"? There was one person. Aware of the news coverage as well as the rumblings at GWDC, Mr. Bob Stoddard, a staff member at GWDC, seized on the concept with enough enthusiasm to mobilize the entire community. First, Mr. Stoddard convinced GWDC to allow him to develop the building as a performing arts center. While researching the theatre in the library, he discovered that both the Grand Opera House and the *News Journal* had a 100th birthday in 1971. He approached John Craig, assistant editor of the *New Journal,* with the idea of a joint gala birthday party, and found a willing partner. The gala would serve as a trial balloon to see if the community would accept the rundown theatre as a performing arts center. Delaware State Arts Council's leaders, Polly Buck and Craig Gilborn, wholeheartedly agreed that Delaware needed a performing arts center and agreed to provide financial assistance. Fred O'Donell, President of the Wilmington Savings Fund Society, the bank which owned a large part of the real estate on the Opera House block, offered leadership and support.

In the fall, after a visit to the Springer Opera House, a 19th century Opera House in Columbus, Georgia, leaders were convinced that the revitalization of the Opera House as a center to serve local performing artists was a sound idea. They began organizing a centennial celebration which would excite public attention and initiate wide community support. The original leaders took a leading role by making generous contributions and urging other community leaders to do the same.

As the fall progressed, support increased. Craig Gilborn met with representatives of twelve local groups, including the Delaware Symphony, the Opera Society, the Lyceum Players, and the Drama League in order to interest them in participating in the gala.

The gala was made public in November when Governor Peterson, County Executive William Conner, and Mayor Haskell announced plans for the gala with the hope that "the old lady of Market Street could once more become a cultural center for the State."

As Governor Peterson explained, the need was intense; Delaware lacked a performing arts center:

Now that the arts council has been established, it has become increasingly apparent that in spite of the fine work of the council and of the richness and vitality of our own cultural heritage and high quality of our performing arts groups, there is still one missing major ingredient. As Governor of this State, I have long been concerned that Delaware is without a center of the performing arts. Certainly the people of this State need and deserve a first-class performing arts center.[5]

While community groups made elaborate plans for the gala, the Grand continued to show its regular movies. *Slaughter* and *Boxcar Bertha* were featured during the week of November 17; the week of December 7 brought *Mission for a Killer*. Just ten days before the gala, after the Sunday performance of *Shaft* and *A Stranger in Town,* the theatre was closed. In the mere ten days before the gala the badly mutilated theatre had to be repaired; thirteen performing groups had to rehearse and co-ordinate their efforts.

On Monday, the day after the theatre closed, volunteers spent the entire day removing the huge movie screen which had been attached to the stage. By Tuesday the old orchestra pit on the stage was covered with lumber. By Wednesday the stage floor was painted. Over the weekend new lighting, which had been borrowed from the Playhouse, was installed. Other improvements including placing slip covers over the badly mutilatd seats, dusting, cleaning, vacuuming, and installing portable toilets in the basement. On Tuesday and Wednesday continual dress rehearsals were scheduled.

December 22, 1971 was a glorious evening in Wilmington. Exactly 100 years after leading Delawarians danced at the opening ball of the Masonic Temple, some 1200 Delawarians again flocked to their Victorian Opera House. Horsedrawn carriages trotted down Market Street from the duPont Hotel carrying community and government leaders and members of the Victorian Society in America. The official program opened with a promenade of Victorian Society members in Victorian costumes. Don Dunwell was Master of Ceremonies. Walter Nelson spoke about "One Hundred Years Ago Tonight." Bill Frank adressed the audience on "Famous Thespians at the Grand." Performances by some ten local groups and the Mendelssohn Club of Philadelphia comprised a program that lasted nearly four hours. At midnight an immense cake was rolled onto the stage and champagne was passed through the audience. Everyone toasted the second 100 years of the Opera House. The evening concluded with dancing on the stage.

It was an electric night. The audience left after four hours, tired but excited by the potential. Project leaders had a clear message; a large portion of the general public was enthusiastic about converting the old downtown theatre into a viable center.

The Gala, as it was popularly labelled, had established the first famous moment of the centennial rebirth. Each of the key moments in the centennial development became a dramatic event in itself— filled with excitement and enthusiasm.

After the gala the Opera House slipped out of public view. Rumblings about its demise were often heard. Actually, behind the scenes, an executive committee led by newly elected president William Prickett was diligently working to create a charitable corporation which could receive title to the building. The Masons who had been gravely concerned about the condition of the building could not undertake renovation because of tax and financial problems and their inability to obtain funding from governmental sources. Therefore the Masonic Hall Company, encouraged by leading Mason Everett Ragan, and the Executive Committee, agreed a non-profit corporation had to be established. Mayor Tom Malony provided the first governmental support by allowing the building to be transferred from the Masons to the City and in turn from the City to GOH, Inc.

By the conclusion of the interim thirteen months (December 1971—January 1973) a new non-profit organization, Grand Opera House Inc. with a 60 member board, had been created and title to the building had ben transferred from the Masons to the new corporation. According to the terms of the of the agreement, GOH, Inc. promised to operate the building as a performing arts center, to

146

invest at least one million dollars in the building within four years, and to maintain the Masonic meeting and recreational facilities.

The interim year had strengthened the committment of project leaders and broadened the base of support. Performing arts enthusiasts, led by Dr. Lawrence Wilker, a professor in the Theatre Arts Department of the University of Delaware, now realized that the Opera House could serve not only local groups but outstanding international companies as well. Urban developers recognized that the Opera House could be a focal point for the renewal and revitalization of the City. As in the 1870s, the theatre occupied an ideal location within the City; it was the center of the first block of the proposed new mall; it was within a few blocks of extensive parking space; and it was directly across from the new governmental complex. Preservationists saw the significance of rescuing a major Victorian building from decay or demolition.

Once again the site of 818 Market Street had been selected as the site of Delaware's performing arts center. In the 1870s the site committee had spent one year selecting a lot. In the 1970s the steering committee spent about one year to gain possession of the site once the Gala had proven it was correct. The new board issued a challenge to the community. In the words of President William Prickett:

The second century of the Grand Opera House should continue to carry out the vision of the early Masons who built the House. However, to make the foregoing possible it will be necessary for those in the present generation to equal the generosity, industry and foresight of those who came before. If this challenge is met, the present and future generations of Delawarians are sure to be the benefactors since not only will the Grand Opera House become a center for the performing arts for Delaware but another step will be taken in the revitalization and reconstruction of the City itself.[6]

SCENE TWO

PREPARATION FOR BUILDING

Although the site had been chosen, the building could not be restored immediately. As Bill Prickett so wisely advised, in order to capitalize on the community excitement, the potentials of the GOH as a center for the performing arts had to be demonstrated to the public immediately.

Despite the changes made before the gala, the theatre was in a deteriorated condition, and certain preliminary changes were necessary to make the theatre operable. The seats were almost totally destroyed; the red satin wall covering was stained and torn; there was inadequate house lighting and no stage lighting; and a flat ceiling had been installed 10 feet below the original frescoed ceiling. During January and February a preliminary cleanup was accomplished in record time. All the old seats were "junked" and replaced with seats donated by the owners of Loews Aldine next door. Some $13,000 of electrical work was installed. The walls were stripped of their satin and cotton padding and painted white. Lighting was installed.

On February 1, the house was rededicated with an inaugural concert by the Delaware Symphony. The initial season was a smashing success. Capacity crowds attended the Cleveland Symphony, Vienna Choir Boys, Berlin Concert and Choir, and the Harkness Ballet. After the Berliners concert, the newspaper reported: "The GOH should continue to bring to downtown Wilmington such attractions as last night's offering, the Cleveland Orchestra and other excellent events being offerred in the future." [1] When the Harkness Ballet appeared, a dance critic commented: "ballet history was surely made in Delaware last night." [2]

Project leaders were excited by the community's enthusiasm, but the picture was vague. Yes, Delaware was a State without a performing arts center. There were thousands of its citizens eager to have a center and willing to come to downtown Wilmington. But what events did they want to see? Would they contribute to the center? What would it cost to run the theatre? Physically, what could be done to the building?

Inspired by the outstanding support, GOH, Inc. not only planned a full 1973-1974 season but also explored long-range plans. Cresap, McCormick, and Paget were hired during the summer of 1973 to estimate costs for operating the theatre on an annual basis. Community Resources, Inc. was hired to provide fund raising council about potential contributions to the Opera House. Both reports concluded that the project was feasible.

During the spring the long range planning committee, composed of Joe Angell, Jr., Pete Larson, William Prickett, Kitty Reese, Bob Stoddard, Tom Watson, and Larry Wilker, began investigating architectural possibilities. Questionnaires were sent to more than forty-six architectural firms which specialized in either theatre or restoration. Some twenty-six interested firms were then evaluated by the committee according to specialty, experience, proximity, acoustical expertise, and other key factors. Between May and August the group was limited to thirteen firms. The committee met with the architects and visited examples of their work.

In September 1973, GOH, Inc. signed a contract with Grieves, Armstrong-Child, and Baird—three architects from individual firms teamed up to provide expertise in all areas. James R. Grieves of Baltimore led the team. With his strong background in general restoration and organization, Mr. Grieves would provide the general overview necessary for the difficult technical and aesthetic problems. Mr. Grieves had experience in renovations at the Brandywine River Museum and the town houses on Society Hill in Philadelphia. Lale Armstrong of New York's Armstrong-Child, who had experience in theatre architecture, had worked in several theatre restorations. Steven Baird, the preservation and cast-iron expert, had worked on similar buildings, one in his native Salt Lake City. According to the terms of the contract, the architectural work was to involve the theatre, stores and second floor offices—not the Masonic space. The work was divided into two phases: Phase 1—measured drawings of the existing building and Phase 2—a program and design for additions and alterations.

While the long range building plans developed, a greatly expanded program continued to provide Delawarians with outstanding entertainment. The four-event Grand Music series opened brilliantly with the Virtuosi de Roma and included the Budapest Symphony, Van Cliburn, and Music from Marlboro. A Grand American Dancers series featured the Murray Louis Dance Company, the Joffrey II Ballet Co., and the Alvin Ailey City Center Dance Theatre. In order to please a variety of tastes, a Grand Jazz Festival presented Two Generations of Brubeck, Nina Simone, and the Preservation Hall Jazz Band. The Experience of Shakespeare featured three films and a performance of *Measure for Measure* by the City Center Acting Company. The Delaware Symphony held its seven-event series at the Opera House. The Wilmington Opera Society presented *Tosca*. A foreign film festival completed the picture. In order to insure that the programming be continued on the

Van Cliburn

same excellent and professional level, in April 1974 Dr. Lawrence Wilker was hired as full-time executive director.

The architects submitted a set of measured drawings, illustrative plans, and section of the proposed changes, a statement of design considerations and a colored sketch of the ceiling to the Opera House in February 1974. The plans were based on several basic design considerations: the theatre's strategic position in the redevelopment of Wilmington, the historical value of the building, an update of the building with regard to fire protection, easy access and egress, the economic and technical requirements of the theatre, the need to improve the shops and create new ones, and the need to maintain the separateness of the Masonic spaces.

150

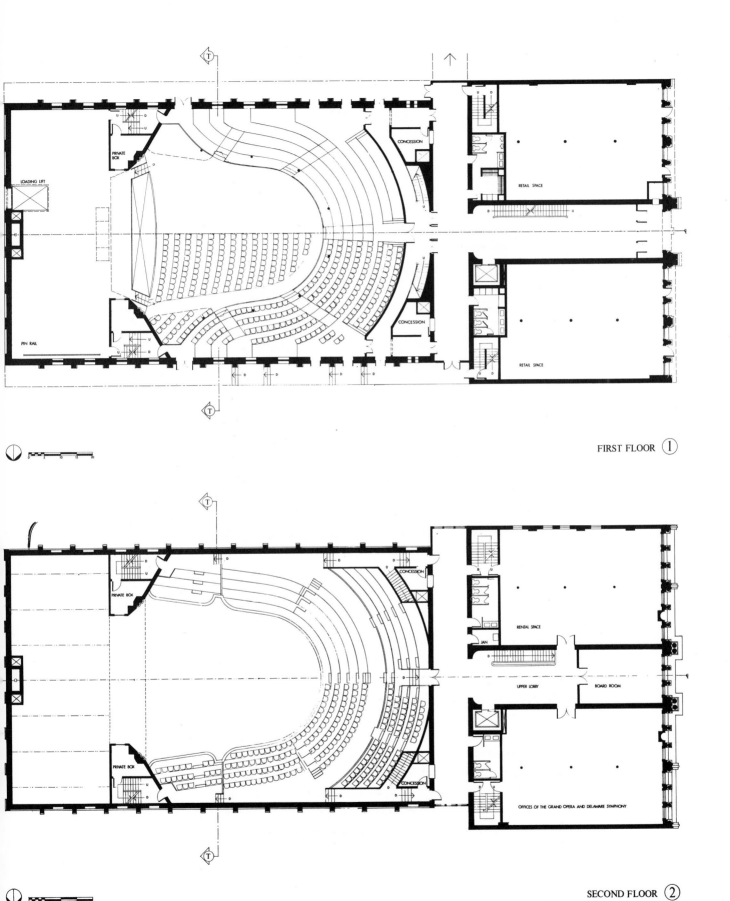

PRIVATE BOX

LOADING LIFT

PIN RAIL

CONCESSION

CONCESSION

RETAIL SPACE

RETAIL SPACE

0 5 10 15 20

FIRST FLOOR ①

PRIVATE BOX

PRIVATE BOX

CONCESSION

CONCESSION

JAN

RENTAL SPACE

UPPER LOBBY

BOARD ROOM

OFFICES OF THE GRAND OPERA AND DELAWARE SYMPHONY

0 5 10 15

SECOND FLOOR ②

The basic design conception was to restore the Victorian theatre in the context of a technically sound 20th century theatre. Therefore, all forms of restoration would be used—preservation, restoration reconstruction, and, where necessary, new construction. For instance, in the theatre the original seating plan as well as the spirit and form of the entire theatre would be adhered to as closely as possible. However, the backstage and basement areas would be totally new construction. Parts of the original lobby would be restored but a new cross-axial lobby would be constructed in order to alleviate the flow of traffic problem.

Grieves, Armstrong, and Child had suggested that the actual construction of the project could best be managed by a construction manager who would act as the GOH, Inc.'s agent. Therefore, as soon as agreement on the basic design priciples was reached, the building committee interviewed prospective construction managers. By the end of March 1974 the firm of John E. Healy and Sons had been selected from a group of six interested firms. The firm was hired in order to co-ordinate all the construction processes and to make sure that all aspects of the work were covered by trade contracts. Grand Opera House Inc. made all contracts directly with the trade contractors; Healy's position was advisory. The initial phase of the construction manager's work was to compile a detailed cost estimate of the project. On April 19, 1974 John Healy presented a preliminary estimate of $3,133,063 for remodeling and restoration. The estimate was based on preliminary design drawings, detailed inspection of the building's mechanical and electrical systems, and on conferences with the architects, consultants, and trade contractors.

After Opera House leaders added another $100,000 of contingency funds, $300,000 operating funds through fiscal 1977, and $100,000 shrinkage, the Board of Directors voted to proceed with the $3.8 million restoration. The architectural team and construction manager agreed that the restoration should be done in one period rather than in segments. Alternating the restoration over two years or more would greatly increase the overall costs due to the inflation of construction materials and the increases for the added "start-up costs." The Board of Directors voted to complete the construction drawings by spring 1975 and to close for one full year of restoration.

The process of determining the feasibility of the project, selecting an architect, and finding a construction manager had taken approximately fifteen months (January 1973—April 1974), a time element not much longer than the twelve months spent in 1870. In 1870 the preparation for construction included four months in choosing an architect, three months in selecting contracts, and a few months while the site was cleared.

SCENE THREE

FACADE

A parade of government leaders and Opera House enthusiasts led by a highschool band is marching down Market Street to the Opera House on July 1, 1974. Several hundred noontime strollers join the parade at the Masonic Hall for a brief program, which features speeches about the significance of the cast-iron façade, and the theatre itself. Portions of the modern storefronts are removed revealing two slender cast-iron columns to the left of the front entrance. The program climaxes when Mayor Thomas Maloney climbs on a fire engine ladder to the roof of the theatre and paints the all-seeing Masonic eye on the central pediment of the façade. The cause for all this celebration? Restoration of the façade is imminent!

154

The dream was translated into a reality by the extremely generous contribution of the Longwood Foundation, a civic-minded local foundation, which pledged $250,000 outright and another $750,000 at the end of the campaign if the goal could be reached. Board Chairman John Craig, who had begun efforts to raise the necessary funds several months before, was largely responsible for interesting the foundation leaders in the potential of the Opera House.

In order to begin restoration of the façade immediately, a "fast track" system was adopted. In a fast track system, phases of the design, bidding, and actual construction processes are done in an overlapping rather than an end-to-end process. A few systems are designed and bid; while construction on these systems begins, other systems are being designed. By overlapping the systems, the time lapse is shortened. For instance, when the construction drawings were being finalized in July, demolition was underway. While the cast-iron pieces were being produced, bid pacs for roof slating were out for pricing.

A few days after the symbolic beginning, restoration actually began under the direction of chief restoration architect Steven Baird and construction manager Jim Healy. Temporary wood storefronts were installed and the existing modern storefronts were demolished. On July 9 the movie marquee was removed. Demolition proved helpful by providing additional information. It exposed portions of the elegant cast-iron arches and columns of the original façade. The shops on the north side were in relatively good condition, but the shops on the south side were missing many pieces. Fortunately, at least one of every original cast-iron arch, column, molding, and trim still existed. In early August designated pieces of cast-iron were unscrewed from the façade and were shipped to Rummell Pattern Makers in Salt Lake City. Rummell used the originals to make wood patterns which were later made into sand molds. During the week of October 14 the new cast-iron pieces arrived in Wilmington and was installed. Although each of the columns appears to be one piece, each is composed of smaller parts welded and screwed together.

The mansard roof needed extensive repair. Since the three cupolas had burned during the early 20th century, three new cupolas had to be built—the central one thirteen feet by ten feet, the others

ten feet square. Both central dormer windows were rebuilt in their original oval shape. After the entire roof was reslated in a pattern of hexagonal and straight slates, an elaborate grillwork was installed around the entire roof.

While work on the storefronts and roof proceeded, the central portion of the building was cleaned and painted. Most of the cleaning was done with wire brushes, but some sandblasting was done on the storefront level below the cornices. The beautiful off-white had been documented by the original specifications and by paint anaylsis of the seven existing layers of paint on the façade. Despite small variations in color, the intention had remained consistant, *i.e.,* to imitate the off-white color of stone.

In mid-October the scaffolding used in the restoration was removed so that it would not interfere with the installation of mall

*Leontyne Price signing autographs after her concert at
The Grand Opera House*

paving. The façade was dedicated on November 20 by Leontyne
Price, who began her performance with a rendition of "The Star
Spangled Banner" while the Delaware flag was raised on the new
flagpole outside. After the performance the audience stood on the
mall gazing with pride at the transformation of the Grand Opera
House, completed in five short months.

Numerous details like the elaborate grillwork on the mansard
roof and the cast-iron bases for the columns delayed work for several
months longer. The final detail, the central cast-iron arch for the
central doorway, was not installed until June 1975. However, the
entire façade now stood as a symbol of the success of the project.
Furthermore, by completing the major portion of the façade in late
1974, the Opera House had co-ordinated its efforts with the construction of the 8th-9th Street block of the new mall.

Costs of the 1974 work were much higher than the original work
had been. In 1871 the cast-iron façade was contracted to Royer
Brothers for $16,810. In 1974 the cast-iron plus labor was some
$82,000. Originally, Gault and Sons were paid $250 for slating the
roof. In 1974, roofing, flashing, and slate were $15,000. Rebuilding
the cupolas cost an additional $12,313. Cleaning and painting cost
$16,000. The total restoration, cost $284,770.74 was under budget.

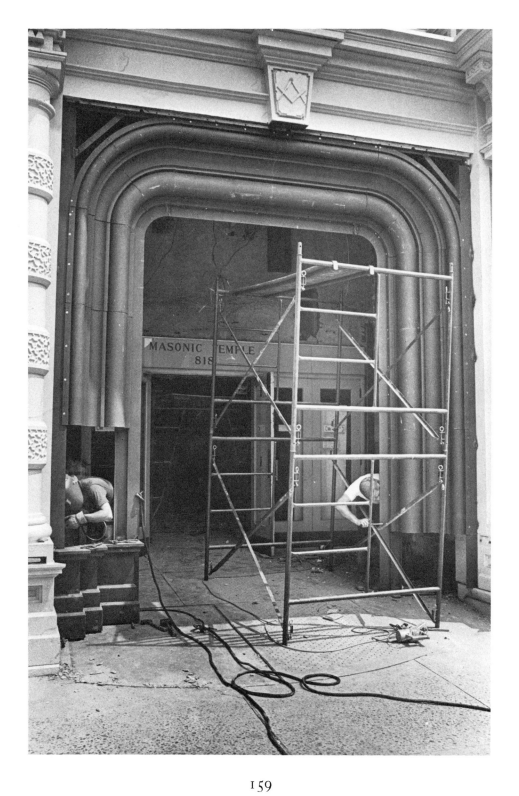

SCENE FOUR

JUGGLING

The 1974-1975 season might best be described as a juggling act. The jugglers, otherwise known as the staff and executive committee of GOH, Inc., used their individual talents and enthusiasm to perform a variety of feats. They directed music and dance programs, façade restoration, fund raising, architectural investigation for final plans, and historical research, While the jugglers tossed these activities about, the public waited to see if the next act would materialize.

Although the restoration would not proceed unless the $3.8 million goal was reached, architects, contractors, and researchers made plans for the "go ahead." Drawings were refined, budgets finalized, bid pacs prepared, and the activities of some twenty-six trades scheduled. Co-ordinating the historical viewpoint with architectural, theatrical, structural, mechanical, electrical, and acoustical viewpoints became a major task.

In August, 1974 the first of the final phase meetings between the architects and Historical Restoration committee, which had been researching the building since 1973, was held. The basic philosophy was clearly emphasized: to restore the house and as much of the lobby as possible to its original 1871 state while making the stage and backstage areas as technically perfect as possible. While restoring the theatre itself, the goal was to provide an attractive, elegant center for the performing arts in a theatre which would accomodate and enhance performances.

During the finalization of the plans, several key historical areas were of major concern: the ceiling, the seating, the windows and the stage area.

Ceiling

When the theatre was acquired in 1971, there was a flat ceiling some ten feet below the original. This fire-resistant, flat ceiling had been installed in the 1940s when large structural trusses had to be placed beneath the original ceiling for support. The restorationists insisted that the ceiling be raised to full height. From a historical point of veiw the frescoed ceiling was significant because it had been the "crowning glory" of the décor. Mr. Grieves's engineers had the structural imagination to design a system of support to the Masonic rooms using smaller beams than the former trusses. Technically the ceiling could be raised since the new beams would only occupy some two feet of vertical space. From an acoustical point of view, raising the height was a risk since the 1971 acoustics of the hall were considered to be very fine.

The consensus was to raise the ceiling. The first complication arose when the lighting consultant Roger Morgan advised that for ideal front lighting on the stage, a continuous lighting position should be installed in the ceiling to hit the performers at a 45° angle. If this lighting position were installed, it would cut right through the heads of the frescoed figures and effectively destroy the ceiling's beauty. The issue was resolved by a unique compromise. The architects designed an elevator type platform, which operates like stage rigging, on which to mount the lights. Before a performance the lights can be adjusted by lowering the platform and reaching it by ladder from the balcony. During a performance the platform is raised to a position neatly within the ceiling; only the front edge turns down about thirty inches to act as a light slot. The ingenious device which was dubbed "Kitty's Catwalk" (in honor of Kitty Reese one of the chief historians) solved the dilemma by allowing the historians to have their fresco and the theatre to have the finest lighting facilities.

The issue of whether to fresco the ceiling or whether to use a painted canvas was continually debated. Evidence of how the original ceiling had been executed was conflicting. In the final analysis, direct frescoeing proved far too expensive; so the historical research committee elected to have the design painted on canvas which could be adhered to the ceiling. The final compromise on the ceiling concerned the placement of the fresco. In order to present the fresco to best advantage the positioning was altered: a border was placed near the front so that the catwalk would not interfere with the main panels.

Windows

Originally fourteen windows lined each side of the theatre and created a meeting-house atmosphere. Historians felt the windows should be restored in order to preserve the scale and integrity of the atmosphere. However, the acousticians were adamant about not opening all these recesses to the noise of the downtown area. Price also was a deterrent since original estimates claimed authentic windows might cost an additional $800 each.

Mr. Grieves, who felt strongly about the importance of the windows, solved the acoustical problem by designing windows that would be recessed only about one half of the exterior wall thickness. Glass panes with wooden shutters behind them would be installed to make the windows look real on the inside but, since the wall would not be fully demolished, no windows would show on the outside. The compromise allowed the ambience of a meeting house to be maintained without detracting from the technical excellence of the theatre.

Seating

Innumerable debates concerned the seating layout as well as the chairs themselves. Historical researchers, were anxious to use the original 1871 seating plan which featured a center aisle and horseshoe parquet circle. But the economics of running an efficient theatre necessitated installing the maximum number of seats commensurate with comfort. Perhaps the center aisle would eliminate too many seats. Perhaps the old seating layout and the exit plan would not meet the more stringent fire codes.

After careful study of four alternate plans, all parties agreed that the total number of seats in each plan would not vary significantly because without a center aisle the rows would have to be set farther apart in the continental style. The horseshoe could be modified to provide good seats from all sections. Because there was no compelling reason not to use the original plan, the group elected to use it in order to preserve the character of the 1871 house.

The nature of the seats themselves continued to be a source of debate until October 1976, when the bid pac for seats was submitted. Although researchers knew that cast-iron chairs had been produced by Bartlett and Robbins in Philadelphia, no patent or accurate historical descriptions could be found. The committee did locate the patent for the Koechling chair which had been the Mason's second choice and was leaning towards using this model. But consistent with the goal of making a technically excellent theatre, the chief requirement of the seats was comfort. The architects strongly advised using a chair that existed and could be copied. When Stephen Baird located a cast-iron chair made in Philadelphia in the correct period, the committee accepted it. But, when the model was discussed with a prospective manufacturer, the cost became prohibitive: more than $115 per chair. So the final compromise in chairs was made. Standard chairs of wood backs and sides would be used with cast-iron replicas of side posts and seat backs. By the end of November, American Seating Co. had been selected to produce the chairs at $79-$88 each.

Stage Area

Originally, two boxes lined each side of the stage. The historians wanted to restore the boxes, since they were a typical feature of Victorian stages. But they would have severely blocked the entrance to the stage wings and would have been a barrier for dance troupes. By occupying too much room on stage, they would thereby limit the usable stage space. After several months the groups agreed to build very small boxes which were more like stage sets in order to create a Victorian ambience without hindering performances.

Finalizing the plans involved many areas besides the theatre. In the huge open basement, which was essentially wasted space, draped blankets separated the men's and women's spaces; one toilet existed for an entire symphony orchestra. The basement had to be completely renovated in order to provide the facilities necessary.

A new "connecting link," was another area. The entity called the Grand Opera House is two distinct buildings: a Market Street office building with the ground floor lobby, and the King Street building with the theatre. Originally, the King Street building was connected to the Market Street building by a third brick section, which filled a portion of the space between the two buildings but left almost an equal amount of space unused. Utilizing the wasted space, the architects designed a new connecting link which could serve as a new crossaxial lobby, and could house restrooms and mechanical equipment not in the 1871 theatre.

The commercial space also had to be developed. Recognizing the Masons' wisdom in providing this source of income in their building and the importance of the commercial space to the rede-

Dance Theatre of Harlem

velopment of the city, Grand Opera House Inc. made plans to prepare these spaces for tenants.

While the final plans were being formulated, Mr. Healy continued to organize bid pacs. Because of the increased specialization of the building industry, the work was divided into more than twenty-six bid pacs. Originally there had been only thirteen. The bid pacs were divided into Structural Steel, Miscellaneous Metals, Roofing, Sheet Metal and Wood Blocking, Painting, Historical Painting, Concrete Work and Excavation and Caulking, to mention a few. The mechanical and electrical bid pacs were prepared and bid in January 1975 in order to test the accuracy of the estimates and to get long term delivery items ordered. Both bids came in under budget. The structural steel, concrete, miscellaneous metals and masonry were accepted by April.

Meanwhile, the music and dance series continued to be supported enthusiastically. The audience was expanded by introducing: a travelogue series, composed of films and lectures; a children's series featuring the Paper Bag Players, Lottee Goslar and Peter Pan done by the junior division of the Wilmington Opera Society. Delaware Symphony and Wilmington Opera Society productions brought still more people. The public was enthusiastic about the Opera House. An Opera House Guild, organized by Nikki Castle, began utilizing the volunteer hours of more than 100 men and women. Concurrently the fund raising campaign, which had begun so successfully with the Longwood contribution, gained momentum slowly. Using all the enthusiasm and talent of the dedicated executive committee members, John Craig organized a superb campaign. In the fall, with the leadership of County Executive Melvin Slawik, New Castle County Council gave the next major gift, $150,000. In January 1975, with the encouragement of Governor Sherman Tribbett

The Paper Bag Players

Boston Symphony Chamber Players

and Senators Don Isaacs and Sherman Webb, the state legislature provided an immense boost by voting $1 million in matching funds if the total could be reached. By February 17, the campaign had raised $3,100,000 from 562 contributors, including the $1,750,000 to be donated at the conclusion. With this solid base of support, the campaign went public.

During the end of February and the month of March, approximately 100 new people contributed to the campaign each week. The total funds increased some $30,000 per week until the last week in March when $64,000 was raised. In early April, when the campaign "took off," the number of new contributors per week jumped to over 300. In the home stretch the community rallied forth to demonstrate it would not let the project fail: in the final three days of the campaign, 610 people brought the grand total to $3,809,000. Increased support during early May increased the total even more.

In another dramatic moment on May 1, 1975 Chairman John Craig announced before an enthusiastic gathering that the goal had been reached and restoration would begin immediately. The theatre would be closed for one year and would re-open on May 1, 1976. During the 1975-1976 season, Grand Opera House would sponsor a music series at Salesianum High School.

SCENE FIVE

MONTHLY PROGRESS OF THE RESTORATION

The proclamation had been issued: A RESTORED THEATRE WILL BE REOPENED ON THE FIRST OF MAY. In order to complete the immense job in twelve months, Grand Opera House, Inc. placed enormous responsibility on three key individuals: Fred Fishback of Grieves, Armstrong/Child, the chief architect during construction; Jim Healy of J. Healy & Sons, the construction manager; and Chris Hubbard of J. Healy & Sons, the foreman. Fred Fishback acted for the design team. As chief architect during the construction, he followed the day-to-day progress adjusting plans as necessary to meet the unforeseen circumstances occasioned by such a restoration. His prompt information kept mistakes at a minimum and avoided misunderstanding that would delay the construction process. Jim Healy acted as liason with the owners of twenty-six trade contractor firms. He brilliantly supervised the work schedules of all tradesmen so the tight schedule could be met. To Mr. Healy fell the difficult task of holding all costs to their budgeted levels. Chris Hubbard co-ordinated the work of all tradesmen and kept the installation of pieces in proper sequence. His meticulous and conscientious approach assured that the finished product would appear and function as designed.

Under the direction of the construction team, preparatory steps were taken immediately. The stage and basement were cleared. All seats and light fixtures were removed. After the balcony seats were removed, the balcony was protected with large sheets of plywood.

Spring

During the demolition months of May and June everything was removed from the theatre. The flat 1940 ceiling, which was about ten feet below the original ceiling, was removed. The demolished plaster and wood lathing slid down the plywood sheets covering the balcony into the central parquet and were shipped out the rear. The movie projection booth was ripped out to re-open a central entrance to the balcony. Several orchestra floors which had been built through the years to improve the sight lines were removed. The proscenium wall, arch, and panels were removed to improve sight lines. By the first week in June only the balcony, resting on its original cast-iron pillars, remained standing.

Demolition provided information which was valuable to the restoration. The balcony was in worse structural condition than anticipated and would require significantly more work. Beneath the plaster proscenium panels, beautiful frescoed panels were discovered. After careful analysis, the panels were judged to be original, and the proscenium plans were altered to include them. Dressing rooms on either side of the stage and stairs to the original boxes were found, confirming reports and original descriptions of the theatre. Gas pipe outlets were located. The original floor was found several feet below the stage level. During the weeks of demolition, Judy Nerdeg, who had been a key researcher for several years, acted as restorationist to make sure that no historically significant architectural feature was destroyed or overlooked. As architect Steven Baird had predicted, "much of the best information for restoration came from physical evidence of the building."

Summer—June, July, August

As soon as demolition of the theatre was complete in mid-June the complex preparation for the new orchestra floors was begun. Grieves, Armstrong, and Child had designed a terraced, contoured concrete floor which would provide excellent sight lines from all over the theatre. The process began by building wood centering from the basement up to the desired floor level. Plywood forms were built to shape the floor, and steel reinforcing rods for structural strength

169

and electrical conduits for wires were installed. By the beginning of July the forms for the central parquet area were complete. In July the forms for the parquet circle were done. By the beginning of August the concrete was poured in various sections of the orchestra.

In June, while the floor was being prepared, the orchestra pit was excavated, and the surrounding concrete block wall was nearing completion by the end of July. Excavation for the stage elevator was underway. After four months' work the theatre looked quite empty; only the floor was in place.

Demolition was still the major activity in other areas of the building. In order to provide a new cross lobby, the old connecting link was demolished so the walls could be expanded to the full property width of ninety-one feet. During June and early July the entire south wall, floors one to four, was demolished. The walls were in poor condition and causing additional work. Demolition of the north side shops was begun. In the lobby, masonry walls were demolished revealing portions of decorative plaster. In the basement, after some excavation, preparations for the new floor were made.

Fall—September, October, November

During September the twenty-eight original window recesses were reopened part way. By mid-October the windows on the stage were permanently sealed with brick construction. The plaster angels and filigree on the balcony balustrade were removed so that the entire façade of the balcony was returned to its 1871 cast-iron. With the floors complete, attention was turned to the ceiling. In mid-September, as soon as the new floor was poured, a "cherry picker" drove into the theatre and was used to install new supporting beams and to remove the old trusses.

By the end of September the new steel beams were in place. Two old trusses above the stage remained in place in order to support the new stage grid iron. By mid-October scaffolding was built over the entire orchestra and balcony area so that work on the ceiling could be performed. New structural metal lathing was installed until early December when the plasterers began applying the first of several coats. The masonry wall above the proscenium was also under construction in mid-October.

Construction of the connecting link continued. The south foundation wall was built in early September.

Two-thirds of the basement floor was poured by early September. Sewer pipes and plumbing were installed. New supporting beams were set in the north shops where the original columns had been removed to make the space more flexible.

By mid-November the new lobby floors were installed. The fire exit stairways were complete up to the projection booth level. Underpinning of the masonry wall in order to lower the cinema floor was complete.

Winter

Suddenly the restoration which has proceeded smoothly for seven months is floundering. Increased costs threaten to bring the restoration to a premature finish. Throughout the restoration, the board of directors carefully followed its progress and voted changes to the original plans in order to provide the most ideal building possible. The ideas of including special facilities for the handicapped, of developing the commercial space for first class tenants,

171

Opera house may have to trim its sails

By PHILIP F. CROSLAND

Unless the source of an additional $1.5 million is in sight by Dec. 22, restoration of the Grand Opera House may have to stop, according to John G. Craig Jr., board chairman.

The current crisis has been caused by a $500,000 reduction in anticipated income and additional costs of more than $1.27 million.

Craig said the board plans no general appeal, such as the successful drive mounted last year, but will approach sources which didn't respond to the earlier drive.

The largest loss of income was due to a misunderstanding with New Castle County Council, Craig said The Grand had expected $500,000 from the county. Council already has appropriated $150,-000, but informed Craig there is no provision for the additional $350,000 in its fiscal 1976 budget.

In addition, Craig said, some construction contracts have run higher than budget estimates. "In part, this has been due to the fact that as the old building was taken apart, unforseeable structural repairs are required that were not budgeted," Craig said.

"Also," Craig added, "there have been some overruns in phases of the project that had of

opinion

The Grand needs help

At a recent forum on the future of the city of Wilmington, speaker after speaker repeated a theme: Restoration of the Grand Opera House is the key to the revival of the downtown

Opera House dying

Continued From Page One

is just not prudent to o go any further when we do not have the promise of money coming in."

other historic buildings and restored to its former glory.

Its redemption was expected to rekindle interest in the then — shabby area. It would provide a

substantial additional income in a few weeks, the remodeling work may have to be suspended. Even a short halt in the work would throw the project off schedule to the extent that its the bicentennial would have to

board now estimates $1.5 costs. Some of that overrun based on board decisions egan — providing more in the building to insure providing additional serv-sts have been unforeseen:

The Grand Opera House restoration seems doomed

ing available $150,000 in federal funds in December.

blessings that such a development would bring — appears doomed.

including city, state and county governments.

Help Sought for Dollar-Short Restoration

Opera House Awaits 'Pennies From Heaven'

By LARRY NAGENGAST

While waiting for a crucial consultant's report, officials of the Grand Opera House are hoping this week will bring more help for their deficit-plagued restoration project.

The consultants, Wood and Tower Inc., of Princeton, N.J., are scheduled to have their $5,000 report for the city of Wilmington ready on Jan. 26. A favorable assessment is considered a necessity if the project is to overcome credibility and cash problems that now imperil its completion.

ANALYSIS

Meanwhile, bailout efforts are continuing. The project, begun last spring after pledges matched the $3.8 million restoration budget, now suffers from a full-scale financial crisis.

Last month, opera house officials admitted that unforeseen expenses — a not-uncommon problem in restorations — and cost overruns had swollen the project budget to $5.2 million. Also, the failure of pledges to arrive in time

brought a cash-flow emergency, which could shut down the project at any time if there isn't enough money available to pay bills as they come due.

This combination of problems last month brought Wilmington Mayor Thomas C. Maloney to the rescue, with the promise of $150,-000 in federal funds and a willingness to pay for the report by outside consultants.

The $150,000 contribution is a no-strings grant, but Patricia C. Schramm, city planning and development director, notes that bureaucratic red tape is so great

that the money won't be available to pay opera house bills right away.

Mrs. Schramm, who worked out the agreement with the consultants, says the report could resolve the fate of the restoration project, a problem that clearly is more significant than the immediate cash-flow difficulties.

The consultants, she says, will be answering two key questions:

■ What the project will really cost — $3.8 million, $5.2 million, or

See 2 KEY — Page 3, Col. 4

and of converting the wasted basement into an art film theatre were adopted. All of these changes increased the budget. Furthermore, the condition of the building—particularly the balcony and connecting link—were worse than anticipated. Several key trade contracts, particularly the plastering and carpentry, were bid significantly higher than estimated. for some time these increased costs had been lurking in the background like unstated themes. Now they grew to dominate the action. The curtain looked as if it might fall. During December, January, and February the ugly themes of CASH CRISIS, CASH SHORTAGE, dominated the play. Although work in the lobbies and commerical space was halted restoration of the theatre never ceased.

Electrical conduits were installed in the ceiling, balcony, and theatre throughout December and January. The mounting boxes for all electrical fixtures were in place by January 19. The drywall was complete from ceiling to balcony. Plasterers finished the ceiling's final whitening coat by the end of January, and the shop—cast central occulus was installed. In early February the frescoed canvas was attached to the ceiling.

The basement was a scene of great activity in December. By mid-December the electrical vault at the rear of the theatre was poured, and the transformer was lowered into it. The new oil tank was installed under the King Street sidewalk. Throughout the winter plumbing installations for toilets and dressing rooms continued.

Meanwhile, the connecting link progressed. By the end of January the supports for the floor and ceiling of the mechanical room floor were in place.

By mid-February the structural steel for the stairs to the balcony was in place. The proscenium columns which form the arch were installed; spinklers were put in above the stage. A new grid system was installed about the stage.

In February the crisis resulted in a change of leadership. Mr. Prickett and Mr. Craig resigned as President and Chairman of the board. Mr. John Clark assumed leadership of the project. Under Mr. Clark's leadership, several details of the theatre interior were postponed—the paint, carpet, chandeliers, Russell Smith curtain and glass and shutters for windows. All work in lobbies and commercial space was halted. Mr. Clark organized a new campaign to provide funds necessary to open the modified theatre on May 1. Generous support from the city, county, and state governments, the Crystal Trust and Longwood Foundation and hundreds of concerned individuals raised the funds necessary to complete the modified restoration.

Spring

In March the scaffolding was removed from the main theatre. The floor was prepared for the installation of seats by drilling holes through the concrete and installing mounting bolts. By mid-April all of the seats were in place. The new proscenium decor was installed. After the entire connecting link was roofed in mid-March, in mid-April the sound and light booth equipment was installed.

Although the theatre was incomplete, it did recreate the ambience of the 1871 house. As in the original, all the visual excitement was concentrated on the ceiling and the stage. The ceiling, still "the crowning glory," is a "recreation of what could have been there" according to interior designer Dale Amlund's interpretation of newspaper accounts and Victorian design concepts. It is flat but painted to look like a dome. From the central star-studded occulus radiate four large medallions, each with two muses. The border is traced from an original design found on the ceiling during demolition. The warm apricot background casts a glow over the entire theatre.

The imposing proscenium opening glistens with radiance. On either side of the proscenium are two columns and frescoed panels, which are almost exact copies of the panels found during demolition. The new panels are slightly elongated because of the new space. Most of the design has been traced directly from the Victorian panels, despite a few changes made in the bow and french horn. Across the top of the proscenium is a fresco using the same motifs of art, architecture, drama, music, and industry. All portions of the design are co-ordinated through the use of the blue ribbon.

The seats placed in the original seating pattern with its center aisle are standard seats but have been given brown backs and maroon velvet plush coverings. Cast-iron top crests and sides will be added.

But many details are missing. For the entire effect to be captured: the walls must be painted chocolate brown; the proscenium columns marbleized in imitation of scagliola; the boxes trimmed with curtains; chandeliers hung from the balcony balustrade and

174

ceiling; the cavernous window recesses finished with wood shutters and glass panes; the bare floors covered with carpet in the aisles; and the wood coping installed.

Throughout the progress of the restoration local media reported enthusiastically on the restoration effort. But, because so many details are unfinished, the theatre's beauty is not a topic of detailed description (as it was at the 1871 opening). However, echoing the 1871 praise, Pete G. Davis of the *New York Times* describes the newly renovated theatre as "a careful preservation of its original Victorian design . . . when the cosmetic work is completed, the city should have one of the most attractive sites for operatic performances in the country." Paul Hume of the *Washington Post* spoke of the wisdom of renovating the famous theatre.

The two accompanying charts demonstrate that both the original construction and the restoration took twelve months. While it

CONSTRUCTION CHART—1871

Month	Activity
January	Excavation of site and preliminary
February	lumber work.
March	Digging foundation and building
April	foundation walls.
May	Work on structural shell completed,
July	brick exterior walls built, wrought iron braces, carpentry.
August	Cast-iron façade begun.
September	Building roofed in, interior floors, walls, stairways, etc.
October	Gallery floor, interior of theatre plastered, decisions on interior lighting, heating, scenery made, alteration of gas pipes for new lighting system, cast-iron façade continued.
November	Seat and frescoed ceiling contracted, at end of month wood seats are being installed and frescoers begin work on ceiling.
December	Seats are installed, ceiling and walls painted, chandeliers hung, scenery set.

CONSTRUCTION CHART—1975-1976

Month	Activity
May	Demolition (all non-original items
June	are removed) and preparation for new floors.
July	Contoured concrete floor is prepared
August	and poured, orchestra pit is excavated, demolition of old connecting link, basement floor.
September	Window recesses reopened, prepara-
November	tion for new ceiling, construction of new connecting link, basement (sewers, plumbing, electrical, air conditioning equipment installed).
December	Ceiling is completed and the fresco
February	adhered, stage rebuilt, grid installed, sound and light booth begun, dry wall lathing, basement (plumbing, etc.).
March	Seats are installed, balcony im-
April	proved, proscenium boxes and frescoes, sound and light boards installed.

Taylor-Davis Corp., Wilmington—Reinforcing steel for concrete.

DiSabatino & Raniere Const. Co., Wilmington—Concrete Work.

A. Ventresca & Sons, Inc., Wilmington—Masonry Work.

J. R. Clancy, Inc., Syracuse, NY—Stage Rigging and Light Bridge.

American Stage Lighting Co., New Rochelle, NY—Theatrical light fixtures.

Architectural Hardware Co., Wilmington—Hollow metal doors and frames and architectural hardware.

Architectural Woodwork, Division of Brosius-Eliason Co., Wilmington—Wood doors.

Aronow Roofing Co., Camden, NJ—Roofing and Sheet Metal.

Berkey-Colortran, Inc., New York City—Theatrical lighting fixtures.

Berkey-Colortran, Inc., Burbank, CA—Dimming system.

Bruce Industrial Co., Wilmington—Lockers.

Electro Controls, Inc., Salt Lake City—Patch panels.

Erskine-Shapiro Theatre Technology, Inc., New York City—Plugging system.

The Flexible Co., Subsidiary of Rohr Industries, Inc., Loudonville, OH—Coin-operated lockers.

E. F. Higgins & Co., Inc., Middletown, DE—Electrical Work.

Hires Turner Glass Co., Wilmington—Glass and Glazing.

Hoffend & Sons, Inc., Rochester, NY—Stage lifts.

Knickerbocker Partition Corp., Freeport, NY—Metal toilet partitions and shower compartments.

Master Mechanical, Inc., Middletown, DE—Mechanical Work.

Paneltrol, Inc., Elsmere, DE—Miscellaneous Metal Items, including steel stairs.

Richards-Wilcox Mfg. Co., Palisades Park, NJ—Stage folding partitions.

Safeway Steel Scaffolds Co., Philadelphia—Scaffolding.

J. H. Sparks, Inc., Philadelphia—Sound equipment.

Steel Suppliers, Inc., Wilmington—Structural steel, steel joists and metal deck.

Harry S. Lynch Co., Inc., Wilmington—Carpentry Work.

Guy C. Long, Inc., Chester, PA—Lathing, Plastering and Drywall Work.

Union Wholesale Co., Wilmington—Acoustical Ceilings.

Marble Craft Co., Inc., Wilmington Ceramic Tile.

Varsity Floors, Inc., King of Prussia, PA—Stage Flooring.

American Seating Co., Grand Rapids—Theatre seating.

Nolan Scenery Studios, Inc., Brooklyn—Historical Painting.

Hudson-Shatz Painting Co., New York City—Install historic painting.

I. Weiss & Sons, New York City—Stage Curtain.

American Scenic Co., Inc., Greenville, SC—Drapes and traveller rods.

TRADE CONTRACTORS ENGAGED IN RESTORATION OF THE FACADE AT THE
GRAND OPERA HOUSE

Cassidy Plastering Co., Newport—Lathing and Plastering Work.

Corrado Brothers, Inc., Wilmington—Sidewalk Work.

D. W. Griffith, Inc., Townsend—Slate Shingles and Sheet Metal Work associated with gutters and flashings.

E. F. Higgins & Co., Inc., Middletown—Electrical Work.

Hires Turner Glass Co., Wilmington—Glass and Glazing.

N. B. Maccari & Sons, Inc., Wilming—Painting and Caulking.

Savery & Cooke, Inc., Wilmington—Installation of replacement cast-iron, fabrication and installation of pipe railings on roof and cupolas.

Rummell Pattern Makers, Salt Lake City—Fabrication of cast-iron.

CONSULTANTS TO GRIEVES, ARMSTRONG-CHILDS IN INTERIOR RESTORATION

Baird, Young and Jones, Salt Lake City—Consulting Architects.

Roger Morgan, New York City—Theatre Consultant.

K.M.K. Associates, Ltd., White Plains, NY—Acoustical Consultants.

Skarda & Rickert, Inc., Baltimore—Structural Engineers.

Palmer & Clark, Inc., Timonium, MD—Mechanical Engineers.

Carroll Cline, New York City—Architectural Lighting.

is difficult to compare the two processes without precise information on the size of the work force, the length of the working day, and the extent of the work done off premises, it is significant that constructing the theatre from scratch took the same time as restoring it.

In 1871 the interior décor of the theatre both plans and execution, was completed in a relatively short period of time. During restoration work on the interior was continuous after demolition in mid-June 1975 through the early part of May 1976.

"The difficulty of fitting the 20th century facilities into the old box which is not ready for advanced technological systems in large part accounts for the increased time of restoration work," explained construction manager Jim Healy. Consider the lighting and heating as examples.

Lighting

The gaslights of the 1871 house were less complicated than today's electrical lights. In 1871, when the lighting plans were completely altered two months before the opening, Gawthorp Brothers adjusted the gas pipes accordingly. Fitting the advanced 20th century system into the old house became a major problem in 1975. An electrical transformer which could supply more than 1000 amps was installed under King Street. In the basement an electrical room was constructed to house a switch gear panel which distributed power to different areas of the building. For general house lighting, lights were set in the frieze at the periphery of the ceiling. The most advanced theatrical lighting—a Berkley-Colortran computerized lighting system—was installed in the lighting booth. A lighting panel was set on stage right. More than 350 circuits were set on the stage alone. Installation of the complex electrical system continued from July 1975, when electrical workers began putting conduits into the forms of the floor, until May 1976, when the lighting system and the Berkley-Colortran were synchronized. The electrical bid pac was contracted for $330,454. The Berkley-Colortran itself cost an additional $99,150. Numerous other electrical stage lights increased the cost by at least another $62,000. Compare these numbers to the contract for gas lighting—$2,225.

Heating

The story of temperature control follows a similar pattern. In 1870 a simple steam heat system with a boiler produced a comfortable theatre. In 1976 temperature control had become much more complex—not only heating but also air conditioning had to be considered. The complexity of installing the air handling units to circulate air throughout the building cost $707,319.87.

Furthermore, the increased specialization of the building industry adds numerous workers and variables to the process. Consider the ceiling and seating as examples.

Ceiling

In 1871 the ceiling was one of the finishing touches. Although the Masonic Hall Company had contacted Kehrwieder Bros. in October, the firm was not under contract until November 6—a mere seven weeks before the scheduling opening. Apparently the ceiling was not ready for the design even in November since the articles of agreement with Kehrwieder state the work shall be completed in four weeks *"from the time the ceiling is ready."*

During the restoration, preliminary sketches of the ceiling were part of the conceptual plans. The historical research committee interviewed several artists in June 1975 and by mid-July had contracted with Mr. Dale Amlund to design the ceiling and proscenium. Mr. Amlund embellished the designs, perfecting color and interpretation, until December. The cartoons were shipped to Nolan Studios in New York where they were executed on canvas. After nearly two months, the painted mural was shipped back to Wilmington and was installed like wallpaper in a few days. By the time the fresco was installed in mid-February, more than seven months had passed from the date of the contract. In 1871 Kehrwieder Brothers were paid $1,800 for frescoeing the ceiling as well as the walls. In 1976 the design fee was $15,000 and the execution fee $64,850.

Seating

Originally the seats were completed in record time. Although the seats were not contracted until the beginning of November, by the end of the month the wooden seats were being installed. The entire cast-iron order was complete a month after it was contracted; a sample chair had been shipped eleven days after contract. In 1976 major seat manufacturers estimated a minimum of six months production time. The seats were contracted in early October and were installed in mid-April. In 1870 the chairs cost $4.01 cast-iron; 2.28½ wood. In 1976 the chairs ranged between $79-$88.

More than 4.5 million dollars has been invested in the building, but the restored theatre is worth more than bricks and mortar. The performing arts ennoble man; the Grand Opera House, which symbolizes more than a century of performing arts in Delaware, stands as an ennobling symbol of our community.

GRAND OPERA HOUSE
DELAWARE'S CENTER FOR THE PERFORMING ARTS & BI-CENTENNIAL MEETING HOUSE
BUILT BY THE MASONS IN 1871

MAX MORATH
The Ragtime Years
May 1, 1976

Preview concert in honor of
Construction Personnel

GRAND OPERA HOUSE
DELAWARE'S CENTER FOR THE PERFORMING ARTS & BI-CENTENNIAL MEETING HOUSE
BUILT BY THE MASONS IN 1871

INAUGURAL CONCERT

THE DELAWARE SYMPHONY

Van Lier Lanning
Music Director
May 7, 1976

Stefan Kozinski, Piano Soloist

GRAND OPERA HOUSE

Wilmington, Delaware

1871 - 1976

THE LAST OF THE MOHICANS

ACT 5

❦

THE GRAND
EXPERIENCE
1911-1970

In all likelihood, the rededication of the Grand Opera House was the focal point of the second 100 years. In order to emphasize the variety of performing arts experience offered at the Grand, numerous events were scheduled during the opening months. As Opera House leaders had promised, on May 1, 1976 the Grand Opera House was alive with music and drama. Max Morath's *Ragtime Years* was presented as a preview performance to honor the construction personnel who had restored the theatre. "The Ragtime Years" was a hit! The air resounded with laughter and applause. During his curtain calls, Max Morath praised the dedication and interest of the tradesmen in restoring this nationally significant monument. After the concert a celebration party was held.

The Grand Opera House was inaugurated in high style on May 7, by the Delaware Symphony under the baton of Van Lier Lanning. The highlight of this successful concert was the world première of *American Rhapsody for Piano and Orchestra* by Stephan Kozinski. The capacity audience thoroughly enjoyed the music. A festive air dominated as Delawarians praised the newly restored house.

On May 10 Harry James and his orchestra delighted a large number of big band fans.

On May 22 the Philadelphia Dance Company inaugurated the Opera House of dance.

The celebration of the opening reached its climax when the town "hit a frenzied high" in recognition of a gala performance by the Philadelphia Orchestra on May 27, 1976. In the style of the "Grand old days," a parade down Market Street preceeded the concert. Opera House supporters and patrons marched down the Market Street Mall led by members of the Conrad High School Band, Governor Sherman Tribbett, and other governmental leaders. As the procession passed, people joined forces so that by the time the parade reached the front of the hall, a solid mass of humanity filled the Mall.

Inside the theatre Governor Tribbett, Opera House President John Clark, and Vice President Kitty Reese marched up the center aisle escorted by an honor guard to welcome all Delawarians to their newly restored performing arts center. The great assistance of the State and other governmental leaders was praised. The concert featured the première of *Colonial Variants* by Norman Dello Joio. This composition, commissioned by Farmer's Bank in honor of the Bicentennial, was praised for creating the spirit and mood of the American experience.

For the May 28 and 29 concerts the orchestra varied its programs, but *Colonial Variants* was repeated. At the final performance on Saturday, May 29, when the audience gave a standing ovation as each previous audience had done, its enthusiasm was rewarded by an unusual occurrence. Maestro Ormandy departed from custom— he expressed his pleasure in performing at the Grand, and then played an encore: Richard Strauss' *Rosenkavalier Waltzes.*

The Grand Opera House had the privilege of being dedicated to Opera on June 12 by the première of a third original work of art. The Wilmington Opera Society presented Alva Hendersen's *Last of the Mohicans,* written in celebration of the Bicentennial. The première attracted numerous personalities from Washington, New York, and Philadelphia. Numerous commentators acknowledged the significance of this all-American opera based on James Fennimore Cooper's novel.

Throughout June and July the Opera House continued to provide a wide variety of entertainment. Programs included: A Jazz Salute to Clifford Brown by the Wilmington Black Ensemble; a band concert by the New Castle County Bicentennial Band; a program of Jazz Guitars; the ever popular play *1776* by Delaware's Lyceum Players; and Victor Borge. The first annual Delaware Sport's Luncheon was held.

An exciting 1976-1977 season includes a music series featuring Buffalo Philharmonic, The Boston Symphony, and the Los Angeles Philharmonic, Lincoln Chamber Music Society and Julliard String Quartet, a dance series, a children's series. The Wilmington Opera Society and the Delaware Symphony are holding their seasons's performances here. Numerous extra events like renowned pianist, André Watts, and the Vienna Choir Boys will enable the first full year at the restored theatre to be a really Grand year.

My script of *The Grand Experience* is complete, but the drama is not over. The drama of the twentieth century is just beginning. Although there is no finalized script at this juncture, I believe some firm goals are guiding the drama.

While the growth of performing arts experience in Delaware has been stimulated by the Opera House, enthusiasts aim towards a larger goal. Hopefully, some 250 attractions can be presented each season. In order to ensure that the program meets the Delaware taste (a phenomenon that does exist according to historical analysis) an audience development survey designed to give a profile of the audience—its size, composition, and preferences—was conducted. The Opera House has been greatly enhanced and technically improved through the restoration, but it is incomplete. The essential historical ambience is not yet established. Just as Grand Opera House does not present three-quarters of a symphony or actors clothed in half their costumes, I do not believe Grand Opera House, Inc. will leave the theatre unfinished. A small amount of work costing a mere fraction of the entire restoration budget will complete the theatre so it can assume its rank as one of the nation's outstanding Victorian buildings. The commercial space in the Grand Opera House is valuable real estate. By following the wisdom of Delaware forefathers and developing the commercial space, Grand Opera House, Inc. plans to add new dimensions to the city and the building.

Think of this portion of *The Grand Experience* as a drama in its "pre-Broadway," trial state. Its script is still being improved and polished; actors are being added; audience reactions are being incorporated. The success of the drama will depend on Grand Opera House, Inc.'s ability to change with the time, to incorporate new actors and ideas. The Grand Opera House welcomes new actors and ideas. The grand experience is happening now, and the challenge is clear: To create in the twentieth century an experience at the Grand equal in magnitude to *The Grand Experience* of the nineteenth.

CURTAIN CALLS

❧

The restoration of the Grand Opera House began as an "impossible dream." Acknowledging all those who made the project possible would be an overwhelming task; however, at this time, those individuals, whose foresight and dedication are largely responsible for the success of the Grand Opera House, should be introduced.

William Prickett, Esq.
President
1972-February 1976

John G. Craig, Jr.
Chairman of Board
1972-February 1976

John M. Clark
President and Chairman
February 1976

Executive Committee in May 1976

Mrs. Charles L. Reese, III [Kitty], Vice President
Gilbert S. Scarborough, Jr., Vice President
Richard S. Bodman, Treasurer
J. Charles Rosenthal, Assistant Treasurer
Mrs. Stuart B. Young [Toni], Secretary

Mrs. Ben T. Castle [Nikki]
L. C. Dorsey, Esq.
Mrs. Walter Goens [Grace]
Mrs. John Herdeg [Judy]
Mr. Eric W. Kjellmark, Jr.

Mr. Everett Ragan
Mr. E. Everett Ragan
Mrs. Richard E. Riegel, Jr.
Mrs. Nelson T. Shields [Jean]
Mrs. F. Alton Tybout [Hallie]

Board of Directors in May 1976

Charles M. Allmond, III, Esq.
Joseph P. Ambrosino
Mrs. Benjamin M. Amos
Joseph Angell, Jr.
Louis H. Arning
O. Francis Biondi
Richard J. Both
C. Douglass Buck
Robert G. Carey, Esq.
Donald Carpenter
Arthur Carota
Charles S. Crompton, Jr., Esq.
Charles E. Daniels
Mrs. E. Troth duPont
Mrs. W. Coleman Edgar
Sigmund Ettinger
Mrs. Thomas B. Evans
Dr. Ernest M. Fidance

Dale Fields
Mrs. Edwin Golin
Mrs. John Gould
Brian Hansen
Robert E. Hickman
E. A. Hirdler
Donald Horowitz
Mrs. J. D. Issacs
Murray S. Laskey
William Little
Lemuel B. Moore, III
Mrs. Battle Robinson
Mrs. William J. Storey
Richard L. Sutton, Esq.
Thomas Watson
Mrs. Sherman Webb
Harry David Zutz

Staff in May 1976

Lawrence J. Wilker, Executive Director
Robert B. Dustman, III, General Manager
Robert D. Stoddard, Director of Development
Mrs. Maria Conte, Administrative Assistant, Finance
Michael K. Gorman, Technical Director
Michael F. Gallagher, Administrative Assistant, Operations
Ms. Violet L. Perkins, Executive Secretary
Mrs. Nancy Waskiewicz, Assistant Secretary
Mrs. Barbara Cook, Development Secretary
Francis Flannigan, Technical Coordinator
Donald L. Rittenhouse, Director of Publications
A special bow for those who directly helped this book:

Mr. Gilbert Scarborough and the Masonic Hall Company for access to the Masonic records; Rebecca Wilson, hired with funds from the University of Delaware Office of Research Grants; Judy Gould, Judy Herdeg, Susan Poston and Pat diPinto of the Historical Research Committee for research assistance; Fred Fishback, William Prickett and Lawrence J. Wilker for reviewing sections of the manuscript.

And a special thanks for over 3600 contributors to the fund raising

REFERENCES

Unless otherwise noted, all information is based on the Masonic minutes books, checkbooks and a ream of uncollected letters, notes, bills etc. which the historically-minded Masons had saved in their vault.

PROLOGUE

[1] Alfred L. Bernheim, *The Business of the Theatre—An Economic History of the American Theatre, 1750-1932*, New York, Benjamin Blom, p. 6 and Barnard Hewitt, *Theatre USA 1665-1957*, New York, McGraw Hill Book Co., 1959, p. 2.

[2] Jack, Neeson, *The Devil in Delaware*, unpublished Ph.D. thesis, Western Reserve University, p. 1.

[3] *Ibid.*, p. 6.

[4] *Ibid.*, p. 41.

[5] *Ibid.*, p. 42.

[6] J. Thomas Scharf, *History of Delaware 1609-1888*, L. J. Richards & Co., Philadelphia, 1888, Vol. 2, p. 839.

[7] Bernheim, *op. cit.*, pp. 14-15.

[8] Scharf, *op. cit.*, p. 839 and Neeson, *op. cit.*, p. 157-271.

[9] *Wilmington Daily Commercial*, June 27, 1867.

[10] Carol E. Hoffecker, *Wilmington, Delaware, Portrait of an Industrial City 1830-1910*, University Press of Virginia for Eleutherian Mills-Hagley Foundation, 1974, p. 71.

[11] Interview with Dr. Carol E. Hoffecker, June, 1976.

[12] Bernheim, *op. cit.*, p. 19.

[13] Scharf, *op. cit.*, p. 817.

[14] Interview with Mr. Charles Green.

RISE TO GRANDEUR

[1] G. M. Hopkins, *City Atlas of Wilmington, Delaware*, Philadelphia, 1876, p. 14-15.

[2] *Ibid.* and *Wilmington City Directory*, Jenkins and Atkinson, 1876.

[3] Obituary of Charles Carson, *The Sun*, Baltimore, Saturday, December 19, 1891.

[4] *Wilmington Daily Commercial*, August 2, 1870.

[5] Cornerstone ceremony as described in *Every Evening* April 21, 1871 and *Wilmington Daily Commercial* April 20, 1871.

[6] *Delaware Gazette,* December 19, 1871; *Delaware Republican,* December 21, 1871.

[7] Virginia E. Lewis, *Russell Smith, Romantic Realist* University of Pittsburgh Press, 1956, p. 198.

[8] Throughout late October, November and December the local newspapers carried progress reports.

[9] The description of the hall in 1871 is compiled from the *Every Evening,* December 23, 1871; *Wilmington Daily Commercial,* December 23, 1971; *Delaware Gazette,* December 19, 1871; *Delaware Republican,* December 21, 1871 and *Delaware State Journal,* December 22, 1871.

[10] Interview Margo Gayle, President of Friends of Cast Iron Architecture.

[11] Wilmington Board of Trade *Annual Reports* 1867-1873. Wilmington, Del. n.d.

[12] Carl H. Claudy, Introduction to Freemasonry. Volume I Entered Apprentice, Washington, D. C., Temple Publishers, 1931.

[13] *Every Evening* says 1418 seats exclusive of 24 box seats or 1442 total; *Delaware Gazette* 1418 inclusive of 24 box seats; *Delaware State Journal* 1424; *Delaware Republican* 1425 and bills account for 1433.

[14] *Delaware Gazette,* December 19, 1871.

THE GRAND YEARS AT THE GRAND

The Opening

[1] *Wilmington Daily Commercial,* December 23, 1871.

[2] *Every Evening,* December 23, 1871.

[3] *Every Evening,* December 26, 1871.

[4] *Every Evening,* December 30, 1871.

[5] *The Critique,* March 4, 1872.

[6] *Delaware State Journal,* January 26, 1872.

[7] *Every Evening,* February 1, 1872.

[8] *Every Evening,* February 8, 1872.

[9] *Every Evening,* April 6, 1872.

[10] *Every Evening,* February 27, 1872.

[11] Bernheim, *op. cit.,* p. 32-33.

[12] *Every Evening,* February 8, 1872.

[13] *Delaware Republican,* February 1, 1872.

Scene II — Establishment of the Unchallenged Center

[1] *Delaware State Journal,* March 22, 1872.

[2] *Every Evening,* October 22, 1878.

[3] *Every Evening,* September 29, 1883.

[4] *Every Evening,* April 29, 1884.

[5] *Every Evening,* October 4, 1885.

[6] *Every Evening,* October 8, 1872.

[7] *Every Evening,* February 21, 1882.
[8] *Every Evening,* February 4, 1885.
[9] *Every Evening,* May 19, 1888.
[10] *Every Evening,* December 9, 1884.
[11] *Every Evening,* May 9, 1883.
[12] *Evening Programme,* February 4, 5, 1881.
[13] *Every Evening,* June 3, 1873.
[14] *Every Evening,* September 27, 1884.
[15] *Every Evening,* February 28, 1885.
[16] *Every Evening,* November 21, 1885.
[17] *Every Evening,* December 9, 1886.
[18] *Every Evening,* April 21, 1878.
[19] *Every Evening,* September 29, 1877.
[20] *Every Evening,* February 25, 1882.
[21] *Every Evening,* February 23, 1875.
[22] *Every Evening,* October 16, 1880.
[23] *Every Evening,* March 12, 1886.

Scene III — The National Experiment

[1] *Every Evening,* February 9, 1889.
[2] *Every Evening,* April 11, 1889.
[3] *Every Evening,* November 15, 1889.
[4] *Every Evening,* June 5, 1889.

Scene IV — The Multifaceted House

[1] *Every Evening,* December 26, 1891.
[2] *Grand Opera House Programme,* September 12, 1892.
[3] *Every Evening,* January 7, 1897.
[4] *Every Evening,* September 1, 1898.
[5] *Every Evening,* December 26, 1898.
[6] *Opera House Programme,* December 29, 1883.
[7] *Every Evening,* May 12, 1897.
[8] *Every Evening,* September 15, 1900.
[9] *Every Evening,* January 25, 1898.
[10] *Every Evening,* May 23, 1895.
[11] *Every Evening,* October 31, 1893.
[12] *Every Evening,* March 24, 1892.
[13] Excerpted from text of entire speech in Cyrus Adler, *The Voice of America on Kishineff,* Philadelphia, Jewish Publication Society of America, 1904.

Scene V

[1] *Every Evening,* January 27, 1905.
[2] *Every Evening,* February 14, 1905.
[3] *Every Evening,* December 20, 1908.

[4] *Every Evening,* February 1, 1908.
[5] *Every Evening,* August 31, 1909.

Scene VI — The Changing Building

[1] *Every Evening,* December 23, 1871.
[2] *Every Evening,* August 17, 1909 .
[3] Thomas W. Witson, "A History of Electric Service in Delaware," in *Delaware: a history of the first state,* ed. Henry Clay Reed and Marion Bjornson, New York, Lewis Historical Publication Co., 1947, Vol. I, p. 507.
[4] *Every Evening,* September 1, 1888.
[5] *Ibid.*
[6] *Every Evening,* August 26, 1891.
[7] *Every Evening,* August 17, 1909.

INTERMISSION

[1] Scharf, *op. cit.,* p. 754.
[2] *Every Evening,* March 20, 1885.
[3] *Rugby Academy Catalogues, 1872-1887,* select issues.
[4] Charles Reese, Jr. (editor), "Autobiography of Christopher Ward" in *Delaware History,* Vol. XV, p. 7972.

FALL FROM GRANDEUR

[1] *Every Evening,* February 21, 1911.
[2] *Every Evening,* November 12, 1912.
[3] *Every Evening,* December 2, 1913.

RETURN TO GRANDEUR

Scene I

[1] Interview with Eric Kjellmark, 1975.
[2] *Wilmington Opera Society Preliminary Report of Investigation of Rental of the Grand Theatre from Masonic Hall Co.,* 1967.
[2] *Morning News,* August 25, 1967.
[3] William E. Pelham, *Summary of Grand Opera House Study,* 1967.
[4] Bill Frank. *Morning News.*
[5] Governor Petersen. Statement issued at Grand Opera House, November 1971.
[6] William Prickett, *Grand Opera House, Inc.: A Review of Steps to Date and Outlining of Plans to Renovate the Grand Opera House,* November, 1972, p. 12.

Scene II

[1] *News Journal,* February 2, 1973.
[2] *News Journal,* May 10, 1973.

BIBLIOGRAPHY

PRIMARY SOURCES

Grand Opera House Inc. *Correspondence, Minutes, Reports.* 1971-1976.

Masonic Hall Company. *Cash Book.* 1870-1919.

Masonic Hall Company. *Checkbook I.* April 4, 1870- January, 1886.

Masonic Hall Company. *Checkbook II.* 1886-1898.

Masonic Hall Company. *Contract Book.* May, 1873-February, 1887.

Masonic Hall Company. *Journal A.* (Money received and paid to theatre, building, and rents)

Masonic Hall Company. *Ledger A.* (Compilation of tenants and incomes received) 1871-1891.

Masonic Hall Company. *Minute Books.* Volume I—March 22, 1869-January 1888; Volume II—1888-1913; Volume III—April, 1913-September, 1934; Volume IV—September, 1934-1944.

Masonic Hall Company. *Receipt Book.* Volume I—February, 1872-December, 1885; Volume II—February, 1886-August, 1888.

Masonic Hall Company. *Tenants and Accounts Book.* 1884-1930.

Masonic Hall Company. Unbound documents in 36 folders.

Rugby Academy Catalogues. 1872-1877, 1880-1883, 1886-1888.

Wilmington Board of Trade. *Annual Reports.* 1867-1873; 1901-1902; 1902-1903.

Wilmington City Directory. 1869-1873 (Jenkins & Atkinson); 1884-1902 (Ferris Brothers and W. Costa).

NEWSPAPERS

Delaware Gazette. December, 1871.

Delaware State Journal. December, 1871.

Evening Journal. Selected articles from 1967-1976.

Every Evening & Daily Commercial. October, 1871-April, 1910
and selected issues from 1910-1945.
Morning News. Select articles from 1967-1976.
Wilmington Daily Commercial. Selected articles from 1867-1876.

INTERVIEWS

As an active member of the Grand Opera House, I have gained valuable insight from informal talks with leaders of the project: staff, executive committee and board members. However, I have conducted more formal interviews with the following people: Charles Allmond, III, Mason and board member; Joseph Angell, Jr., Local architect and Opera House board member; Steven A. Baird, Architect for restoration; Lester Baylis and Helen Baylis, Descendents of Jesse Baylis; Jim Bennett, Assistant manager Warner theatre; Lewis Black, Former manager Warner theatre; James A. Fine, Jr., Masonic Hall Company historian; Fred Fishback, Architect for restoration; Margot Gayle, President Friends of Cast Iron Architecture; Charles Green, Local historian and Mason; Eleanor Goetz, News writer and Arts Committee member 1965; Michael Gorman, Technical director Grand Opera House; James V. Healy, Construction manager of restoration; Carol Hoffecker, Historian at the University of Delaware; Chris Hubbard, Foreman of Grand Opera House interior restoration; Peter Larson, Director Greater Wilmington Development Council; William Pelham, Local architect; Henry Sholly, Drama/movie critic; Earl Smith, Manager Warner theatre; Robert Stoddard, Original project leader.

SECONDARY SOURCES

Books

Adler, Cyrus, editor. *The Voice of America on Kishineff.* Philadelphia. The Jewish Publication Society of America. 1904.
Bernheim, Alfred L. *The Business of Theatre—An Economic History of the American Theatre, 1750-1932.* New York. Benjamin Blom. 1932.
Brockett, Oscar G. *History of the Theatre.* Boston. Allyn & Bacon. 1968.

Canby, Henry Seidel. *The Age of Confidence: Life in the Nineties.* New York. Farrar & Rinehart, Inc. 1934.

Claudy, Carl H. *Introduction to Freemasonry.* Volume I, "Entered Apprentice"; Volume II, "Fellowcraft"; Volume III, "Master Mason." Washington, D. C. Temple Publishers. 1931.

Conrad, Henry C. *History of State of Delaware.* Wilmington. Published by author. 1908.

Green, Charles E. *History of the Grand Lodge of Ancient Free & Accepted Masons of Delaware.* Wilmington. William N. Cann, Inc. 1956.

Grier, A. O. H. *This Was Wilmington.* Wilmington. News Journal Co. 1945.

Hewitt, Barnard. *Theatre U.S.A., 1655-1957.* New York. McGraw-Hill Co. 1959.

Hartnoll, Phyllis, editor. *The Oxford Companion to the Theatre.* Third Edition. London. Oxford University Press. 1967.

Hoffecker, Carol E. *Wilmington, Delaware: Portrait of an Industrial City, 1830-1910.* Charlottesville, VA. University Press of Virginia for Eleutherian Mills-Hagley Foundation. 1974.

Hopkins, G. M. *City Atlas of Wilmington, Delaware.* Philadelphia. 1876.

Lewis, Virginia E. *Russell Smith, Romantic Realist.* Pittsburgh. University of Pittsburgh Press. 1956.

Neeson, Jack H. *The Devil in Delaware.* Unpublished thesis. Western Reserve University.

Poggi, Jack. *Theatre in America. The Impact of Economic Forces, 1870-1967.* Ithaca, NY. Cornell University Press. 1968.

Pomeroy & Beers. *Atlas of State of Delaware.* Philadelphia. 1865.

Reed, Henry Clay and Reed, Marion Bjornson, editors. *Delaware: A History of the First State.* New York. Lewis Historical Publication Co. 1947.

Scharf, Thomas J. *History of Delaware, 1609-1888.* Philadelphia. L. J. Richards & Company. 1888.

Tilly, Jackson, Kay. *Race & Residence in Wilmington, Delaware.* New York. Bureau of Publications Teachers College at Columbia University. 1965.

Wilker, Lawrence. *The Theatrical Business Practices of William A. Brady.* Unpublished thesis. University of Illinois. 1973.

Wilson, Garff B. *Three Hundred Years of American Drama.* New Jersey. Prentice-Hall, Inc. 1973.

Articles

Chance, Elbert, "The Great Days of Wilmington's Grand Opera House." *Delaware History,* Volume VIII, 1958-1959.
Reese, Charles Lee, Jr., editor, "Autobiography of Christopher L. Ward." *Delaware History*, Volume XV, page 7972.

SPECIFICATIONS

OF

WORK AND MATERIALS

FOR

MASONIC HALL,

WILMINGTON, DEL.

Specifications of material to be furnished and work to be done in the erection and completion of a new Masonic Hall, to be built on Market Street, Wilmington, Delaware, according to the plans and drawings thereof, prepared by

THOMAS DIXON, Architect.

August 1870.

No. 1—GENERAL CONDITIONS.

The Building and all of the various parts thereof, are to be erected and finished agreeably to the dimensions shewn or figured on the plans and drawings, in conformity with the particulars set forth in the following specifications, or manifestly implied thereby and according to the instructions and directions given by Thomas Dixon, the Superintending Architect, or exhibited by the working and detail drawings furnished by him. The drawings and specifications are to be taken together to illustrate and explain each other, and should any thing have been omitted, either in the one, or in the other, which is necessary for the completion of the works agreeably to the manifest intention thereof, the contractor, or contractors, shall at his, or their, own cost, do, find, furnish, execute, provide and complete the same as if it had been more fully described, or specified.

It will be the duty of the Contractor, or Contractors for the respective works, to protect and preserve the same and whatever appertains thereto, and if their work or materials receive injury from any cause, they shall renew, repair, or make good the same, so that at the conclusion of the contracts every part of the building may be complete and perfect; and they shall furnish every reasonable facility to the Superintending Architect to examine and test any of the materials, or work; and it shall be the duty of the Architect to reject any materials or work that may be unsound, improper, or unfit for the purpose, or not in accordance with the contract, and all work or materials rejected by the Architect, shall be removed, or altered and made good by the Contractor, or Contractors, at his, or their, own expense.

The Contractor, or Contractors, shall at all times in his, or their, absence, retain and keep upon, or at the works, a competent and responsible person, or persons as foremen, whose business and duty shall be, to take the general oversight of the works, and, attend to, and carry into effect, any directions that may be given thereon, or in relation thereto.

If, at any time during the progress of the building, any alterations, or deviations, from the plans or specifications may be desired by the Building Committee, and they shall consequently order any additions to the work for which a contract may have been made, or any variations, or omissions therefrom, the same shall be acceded to by the Contractor or Contractors, and carried into effect without in any way violating or vitiating any contract that may have been made, but all such additions, omissions, or variations, or alterations, shall be estimated for, and the value thereof agreed upon and approved by the Building Committee by a written Contract, before the Contractor shall proceed to make any such alterations or deviations.

No. 2—EXCAVATIONS AND FILLING.

Dig out for the basement, cellar, areas, vaults, and foundation trenches, as shown by the drawings: the trenches must be sunk at least six inches below the bottom of the cellar, or basement, or deeper than here specified if it should be required to obtain a solid foundation, and the trenches must be dug of a sufficient width to admit the footings to the foundation walls, as shewn by the drawings.

Sink a pit, or cesspool at the most convenient place, of not less than four feet, six inches diameter, and to go to a sufficient depth to have at least three feet of water in the bottom; wall the cesspool with bricks, and cover it with flag stones at least four inches thick securely fixed.

Fill in and ram solid, the earth around the walls: The sod, or soil is to be taken off under all parts of the new building where there is no cellar, or basement; remove all surplus earth from the premises.

No. 3—FOUNDATIONS AND STONE WALLS.

Put in bottom courses for footings to all of the walls, piers, &c. as shewn by the drawings, to project four inches from the line of wall on each side, to be laid very solid, and build all of the basement, cellar, and foundation walls, as shewn by the drawings, of the requisite thickness and heights as shewn or figured, with the best quality of two man building stone that can be procured in the neighborhood; the stone walls are distinguished from the brick walls on the drawings by color.

The stone in all of the walls must have good bed and builds, and all to be laid very solid, and a sufficient number of headers or through stones used to insure strong and solid work in all parts; all laid in mortar composed of fresh lump lime, and sharp grit sand, mixed in proper proportions to secure strong mortar and to be well tempered. Flagging of six inches thick, set under the brick piers and iron columns of the size figured on basement plan.

No. 4—GRANITE WORK.

There will be a door sill of 7¾ inches x 15 inches, and 3 steps 7¾ inches by 12 inches, to each of the door ways from the side yard to the basement, 3 feet, 4 inches long, and a coping of 7¾ inches x 8 inches: There will be a sill of 5 inches x 7 inches to each of the windows of the basement and principal story, of the length shewn by the drawings: There will be a sill of 7¾ inches x 19 inches to each of the two doorways to King Street, and also to the two doorways to the Dressing rooms. There will be a door sill, plinth and landing, to the main entrance doorway, of the sizes and forms shewn, and a plinth on the top of each of the piers of the basement on which to set the cast iron front; all to be of the sizes and forms shewn, and also a coping of 7 inches x 8 inches to the front areas; the coping at each end of areas is to be wide enough to form a spout stone, and to be properly cut for that purpose; all to be of the best quality Brandywine Granite, fine cut, and set in the best manner.

There must be a stone bond in each of the brick piers of the basement; that is, the piers to support the iron front, and also those to support the floor of the auditorium and gallery, in all cases to be the exact size of the pier: Three stones in each of the front piers, and two in each pier under the auditorium, and a stone on the top of each pier, under the auditorium, of sound "North River flagging," at least 3 inches thick, with proper faces.

No. 5—BRICK WORK.

Carry up the brick walls, piers, chimneys, flues, &c., to the requisite heights and of the thicknesses shewn or figured on the drawings: Face all of the out side walls with a good quality of Red bricks. The King Street front to be faced with good quality of Press Bricks, all of uniform color, and laid with a flush joint neatly trimmed; all of the angles and reveals must be carried up true and plumb; the arches over the openings, and the corbels all properly set, and formed as shewn; parget and clean all of the flues.

The segment arches over the vault under the side walk must be put in with straight hard bricks, set in the best manner, with close joints, and firmly keyed.

All bricks in the walls are to be of good quality, well burned, and hand made, laid in mortar similar to that already described for the stone work; no salmon or soft bricks are to be used in any of the walls below the top of the principal floor: the bricks must all be wet sufficiently to remove the dust of the kiln before laying in the walls, and all of the joints must be filled full, flush and solid with mortar, and work with tight joint.

The walls must be carried up uniformly in all parts of the building, and a proper bond preserved in the work throughout; clean down neatly all of the exterior walls. The brick-layer must attend carefully to securing all stone, iron, or other work to be set, or inserted in the walls.

Pave the side walk on the two streets, the side yards and areas, with good paving bricks, laid in a good bed of sand. Moulded, or splayed bricks must be set on the band course, on the King Street front, between the basement and first story. The brick-layer shall set any Terra Cotta pipes in the wall that may be furnished by the Building Committee.

No. 6—CONCRETE FILLING.

The spaces under the floor of the basement under the stores, and under the rooms beneath the stage, are to be filled solid with concrete, and also between all of the floor scantlings to a line with the top of the scantlings; the concrete to be composed of stone and brickbats broken in small pieces, mixed with gravel and lime mortar made as herein before specified; there must be a sufficient quantity used to cement the entire mass together, and it must be thrown in so as to pack close and firm.

No. 7—GROUTING.

There must be a grouting of lime sand made of the consistency of cream and poured on this concrete along each scantling, until all of the interstices are thoroughly filled.

No. 8—IRON FRONT, COLUMNS, AREA LIGHTS, &c.

The front to Market Street is to be of cast iron, executed in all respects agreeably to the drawings, as will be more fully illustrated by the working and detailed drawings, and directions to be given by the Architect: The iron front is to start on the granite plinths: The sills and risers to the store doors, are to be of iron with Hyatt lights inserted.

The entire front, as shewn by the drawings to the top of the principal cornice, including the Pediment, is to be of iron. The castings are all to be of proper thickness, to secure the requisite strength, and all set up and secured in the most substantial manner, and all fitted and finished in a neat artistic and workmanlike manner. The areas in front are to be set on strong iron bars, and fixed and secured in the best manner.

There is to be a strong iron frame and door set to each of the coal drops to the cellar from the side yards, and also a strong iron frame and cover set in the brick arch over the coal vault under the front side walk, each provided with a secure fastening.

The six columns in the front basement to support the floors above must be 9 inches diameter; and the six in the stores 8 inches diameter, all to have 1¼ inches uniform thickness of metal. The eight columns in the auditorium to support the gallery must be 5 inches diameter, ¾ inches uniform thickness of metal: these columns must be made in the very best manner, of good iron, and to have proper caps, &c. All columns to be delivered at building without paint, free from coal sheet, flaws or laps, for inspection. There must be six cast iron shoes for girders of 10 inches x 15 inches placed over the iron columns of the basement to receive the six columns above. These shoes must be made very strong, of good iron, and 1½ inches thickness of metal and 16 inches long on the bottom, and 12 inches long on the top. There must be a plate of 1 inch thick 8 inches x 8 inches on the top of the columns in the auditorium, all properly adjusted. The top and bottom of these columns must be turned, and the shoes and plates turned up to form perfect bearings.

There will be a wire grating of patent wove wire, set in iron frames, the wire ¼ inch made in the best manner, and set to the basement and cellar window frames, and properly secured.

There will be a cast iron pipe of 10 inches diameter, set, and securely fixed in the ventilating shaft, properly stayed with wrought iron stays, with proper arrangement for inserting smoke pipes; and an iron door and frame 2 feet 2 inches x 4 feet 6 inches set in the shaft in the basement story.

No. 9—CARPENTERS WORK AND MATERIALS.

Prepare and lay joists and girders for the various floors as follows, viz.: The girders all to be of No. 1, Yellow, or White Pine; and the joists for the first floor throughout to be of No. 1, Yellow, or White Pine : The joists for all of the other floors may be of Hemlock, but must be of the very best quality White Hemlock.

The girders for the store floors will be 10 inches x 15 inches, and the one for the floor above 10 inches x 12 inches, and the joists 3 inches x 14 inches and 3 inches x 12 inches. There must be a piece of yellow pine of 2 inches x 4 inches and 2 inches x 3 inches in the second story, firmly spiked to each side of each girder on which to set the joists, in addition to which, the joists must be housed into the girder at the top. The girders for the third and fourth floors will be 4 inches x 8 inches placed so as to form a cap to the stud partitions. The joists for these two floors will be 3 inches x 11 inches, the joists for the Hall in rear of the front building will be 3 inches x 10 inches. These joists all to be backed with the plane, and trimmed and framed where requisite, for stairs, flues and sky-lights; the long trimmers in all cases to be doubled, and a double joist in all cases to be set under the partitions that run with the length of the joist. The header joist for the stairway and skylight openings will be hung to the trimmers in wrought iron stirrups, made of iron ½ inch x 1¼ inches secured in the best manner. These joists will be set on the walls, and girders at spaces of not more than 16 inches between centers. There must be two rows of cross bridging to each set of joists, properly cut, and firmly nailed, and a row of solid bridging of 3 inches x 11 inches cut in over the girders of the second and third stories.

The roof of the front building will have rafters of 3 inches x 6 inches supported on purlines of 6 inches x 14 inches as shewn in section, to be supported by 6 posts, of 6 inches x 6 inches placed over the partitions as shewn. The rafters to be set 2 feet between centers; the front, or Mansard roof, will be framed as shewn by the drawings, with 3 inches x 6 inches scantlings set 2 feet between centers, with plates of proper sizes, securely fixed on the top of the iron front.

Frame properly for the "Lanterne" over the sky-lights as shewn by the drawings.

The joists for the auditorium will be 3 inches x 12 inches set on girders of 10 inches x 12 inches; the joists to be spaced at an average distance of 16 inches between centers, with grades &c., all arranged as shewn by the drawings. The joists for the stage to be 3 inches x 12 inches set on girders of 6 inches x 10 inches; the girders set as caps over the partitions. Joist spaces 16 inches between centers. Frame the gallery or Dress circle as shewn by the drawings, the joists to be 3 inches x 8 inches to 3 inches x 12 inches according to length, set at spaces of an average of 2 feet between centers. The girders to support the gallery front will be 8 inches x 14 inches, formed of pieces cut to the proper curve, cased with boiler-iron, ¼ inch thick on front, and bolted and otherwise ironed to make it very secure.

Frame benches with 3 inches x 4 inches and 3 inches x 6 inches scantling for the different levels, all as shewn; the joists for the auditorium, stage, and gallery, will all be bridged with cross and solid bridging in the best manner; the rows of bridging must be within 8 feet of each other, all firmly fixed and nailed.

The framing for the floor of the Lodge Rooms &c. over the auditorium and stage, and for the roof over this part of the building will be constructed as shewn by the transverse and longitudinal sections. The sizes of timbers, irons, rods, bolts, washers, nuts &c. all as figured on the drawings. The roof trusses are to be placed 10 feet between centers, or one over each brick pier; the 3 inches x 16 inches joists for the floors are to be spaced 16 inches between centers. The timber all to be of No. 1, yellow pine. There must be ten iron rods of ¾ in. diameter extending across the building, one to each pier, excepting the two piers nearest the corners, and a cast-iron plate of proper size on the outside of the pier.

The cast iron shoes to be formed and fixed in the very best manner; the rods, bolts, nuts, &c., all to be of the best quality of iron, and wrought, cut and fixed in the best manner. In addition to the 1½ inch suspending rods shewn, to support the girders of the lodge room floors, there will be three 1 inch suspension rods in each of the cross partitions; that is, 24 of the 1 inch rods securely fixed. The 3 inches x 16 inches joists are each to be hung on a wrought iron stirrup of ¾ inch x 1¼ inch iron.

The roof joists will be 3 inches x 6 inches Hemlock, set 2 feet 6 inches between centers; frame out for the eaves and gable cornices as shewn. Frame for a Lantern over the open space between the Lodge Rooms as shewn; ceiling joists of 3 inches x 8 inches Hemlock to be cut in and secured to the tie beams at spaces of 2 feet 6 inches between centers. The joists of the Lodge Rooms floors will be bridged with cross bridging of 2 inches x 3 inches scantling, 3 rows to each set of joists, to be cut to fit, and firmly spiked to the joists. Dragon ties, or rods of ¾ inch diameter to be put in to form an abutment for the bridging, as will be shewn by a drawing, to be firmly secured by nuts &c. Trim and frame the joists in the rear part of the building, where requisite, for all stair openings &c., and put in double joists under partition, all as herein before specified for front part of building.

Cut and fix ribs of 1½ inch and 2 inch plank to form the Domical ceiling of the auditorium and the Proscenium arch, and the ceiling of the gallery, all as shewn; the ribs to be spread an average of 2 feet apart. All the ceilings will be stripped with oak, gum or white poplar battons of 1¼ inches x 2 inches, spaced 16 inches between centers, and firmly nailed; put in bracketing pieces as shewn in the angles of the Lodge room ceiling.

Provide and set all requisite lintels, bond timbers, wall plates &c. throughout the building; all to be of proper sizes.

The lintels to carry the wall over the sliding doors must be trussed to give it sufficient strength. All of the joists, girders and timbers should be seasoned, and of good quality.

Provide and set in the front basement, including the hall in rear of the front building, and also the basement under the stage floor, scantlings of 3 inches x 3 inches heart yellow pine, thoroughly seasoned, set on bricks at spaces of not more than 6 feet apart; the earth must be removed to a depth of at least 3 inches below the bottom of the floor scantlings.

No. 10—SHEATHING.

Sheath all of the roofs with 1 inch sound seasoned sheathing boards of pine or hemlock, laid with close joints, and even top surface, suitable for tin roof.

The partitions and inside of iron front to be studded with 3 in. x 4 in. pine or Hemlock scantlings, set not more than 16 inches between centers, with double studs for the doors, and trussed, bridged, or braced where requisite.

No. 11—WINDOWS.

Prepare and set to the window openings, including the windows of front basement, and of the basement under the stage, doubled boxed window frames and sashes, of the size and forms shewn; the sash to be 1¾ in. thick, hung on the best 2¼ in. axle pullies, on good American hemp cords, with proper weights. To the windows of the fuel and furnace cellar, beaded frames with 1¾ in. sash.

Provide and set 5 inches by 7 inches heart yellow pine sills for all of the windows where no stone sills have been provided. The Dormer windows on the Mansard roof with blocking, or Dado; under the windows must be built as shewn, sash to be 1¾ inches, double hung.

All of these frames and sashes are to be made and set as shewn by the various drawings, and as more fully illustrated by the full size working drawings.

No. 12—DOOR FRAMES.

Prepare and set to the outside doorway, beaded plank door frames to correspond with the window frames, fitted and secured to the stone sill with transom bars &c., as shewn.

No. 13—CORNICES.

Prepare and set all the cornices as shewn by the drawings, and form the gutters carefully with a proper fall to the conducting pipes. The Mouldings, Brackets, Dentils &c., must all be wrought and fixed in the best manner, and in conformity with the working drawings.

No. 14—FINISHING OF LANTERN.

The Lanterns all to be cased and finished as shewn; the sash to be 1¾ inches double hung and made to move by cords, conveniently arranged to work from below.

No. 15—MANSARD ROOF.

The cornices, angle pieces, mouldings, &c., all to be finished as shewn by the drawings.

No. 16—FLOORING.

Lay the first floor and basement with 1¼ inches, and all the other floors with 1 inch well worked southern yellow pine flooring boards of the best cargo run, properly selected for the different roors, all to be of thoroughly seasoned stuff, and laid when dry in courses and well nailed and cleaned off. Counter ceil over the stage and auditorium with rough boards in the usual way.

No. 17—STAIR CASES.

Build staircases from the 1st to the upper stories and also to the basement, all as shewn by the drawings. The steps to be of white ash, or yellow pine 1¼ inches clear stuff, supported on strong carriages, to be open with 12 inch newells, and 6¾ inch moulded, continued rails, and 2¾ inches turned and moulded balusters, all of walnut, with mitered string, and nosings and scotias to return on the ends of the steps.

Provide and set a rail and balusters around the well opening under the lantern on the third and fourth floors as shewn, and build all the steps, stairs &c., throughout, as shewn, properly skirted and finished.

No. 18—GALLERY FRONT.

The gallery front and private boxes are to be framed, corniced, capped, paneled and finished as shewn, and the orchestra, and front of the stage boarded and capped as shewn.

No. 19—DOOR JAMBS.

Provide and set to all of the doorways 2 in. double rebated door jambs, with transom bars and fan lights over the doors.

No. 20—WINDOW CASINGS.

Case all of the windows with 1 inch jambs and heads, the window boards to be put in after the plastering.

No. 21—ARCHITRAVES, &c.

Prepare and set to all of the windows and door openings, moulded Architraves and bead casings, from 4 inches to 8 inches wide, and window boards and surbases, all as will be shown by working drawings.

No. 21—BASE BOARDS

From 4 inches to 8 inches wide, to be set to the various apartments throughout, to have mouldings from $1\frac{1}{2}$ inches to $2\frac{1}{2}$ inches, planted on top ; All casings, architraves, base boards, &c., to be put up after plastering.

No. 23—STORE FRONTS.

The front windows and doors of the stores will be fitted up with sash, frames, and sash doors all as shown by the working drawings; the doors will be made in two thicknesses of $1\frac{3}{8}$ inch each, firmly screwed together, and to have heavy moulded panels, and hung to the frames with 4 inch butt hinges, 3 hinges to each door and each pair of doors must have two strong flush bolts, and a good strong store door rim lock, and latch, all of the best kind.

The space from the window sill to the Hyatt Lights over the areas, will be filled with sash on the inside, and a patent wove wire in an iron frame on the outside to protect the glass.

There will be light wire screens to set in the store doors and windows to protect the glass, conveniently fixed.

No. 24—DOORS.

The main entrance doors will be made folding, in two thicknesses, of $1\frac{7}{8}$ inch and $1\frac{3}{8}$ inch, paneled as shown, and moulded with heavy mouldings outside, hung on very heavy, strong $4\frac{1}{2}$ inch butt hinges, 3 to a door, and to be provided with heavy flush bolts and a strong rim lock with latch, &c., complete, all of approved quality.

To the doorways from the stage to King St., provide and hang folding doors of two thicknesses ; outside $1\frac{3}{8}$ in. with moulded panels, lined with $\frac{7}{8}$ in. tongued and grooved boards, put on diagonally, hung on strong 4 in. butt hinges, three to each door; and to have strong flush bolts with strong rim locks and good latches. The sliding doors from the Hall to the Auditorium will be 12 feet wide, and 12 feet high, made in two thicknesses of $1\frac{3}{8}$ inch each firmly secured together, paneled and moulded as shown, and fixed on rails and sheaves, in the very best manner, and furnished with suitable sliding door locks and knobs, with stops &c., complete.

The doors from the front vestibule to the Hall to be sash doors, made folding in two thicknesses and paneled, moulded, and to be hung on 4 inch butt hinges, three to each door, hung to open outward, and to have strong bolts, and suitable latches and fastenings.

To the door ways in the basement from the Hall to the rooms, folding doors 5 feet by 8 feet, $1\frac{3}{4}$ inch thick, six paneled, plain raised. The doors to the Dressing rooms &c., in the basement, $1\frac{3}{8}$ inch four paneled plain doors 2 feet 6 inches by 7 feet. To the cellar door ways, suitable batton doors, all hung on suitable and strong hinges, and provided with strong and suitable locks and fastenings.

To the door ways from the vestibule to the Auditorium and to the Gallery, fly doors made folding, light, strong frames, covered with cloth, hung on suitable fly hinges, with springs, &c., all fixed in the best manner. The doors to the various offices of the second and third stories, and the doors to the private boxes, dressing rooms, &c., will be $1\frac{3}{8}$ inch, six paneled doors, 2 feet 8 inches by 7 feet, moulded both sides, all hung on suitable hinges, and furnished with good mortice locks, and proper knobs, &c., complete.

The doors of the Lodge rooms and other rooms on the same floor will be $1\frac{3}{4}$ in. six paneled doors, 3 feet by 7 feet 6 inches, moulded both sides, hung on suitable hinges, and finished with good mortice locks, with knobs, &c., complete.

To the doorways of the Banqueting room and Gymnasium, in the upper story, provide and hang $1\frac{3}{4}$ inch folding doors, 5 feet by 8 feet, six panels (plain,) in each door, hung on suitable hinges and furnished with strong bolts and locks.

The doors of the water closets will be $1\frac{1}{4}$ inch, four plain panels, 2 feet 4 inches by 6 feet 8 inches, hung on suitable hinges, and to be furnished with proper fastenings.

No. 25—GALLERY.

Build a gallery or passage way from one of the rear windows of each store, over the area, to the dressing room and water closet, on joists of 3 inches by 8 inches, floored with 1¼ inch heart flooring, and to have a rail on one side; the joists to be properly cased. The windows opening to this gallery must have three additional lights, to come to the floor, and to have a hood to allow the lower sash to run up for head way.

No. 26—TICKET OFFICE &c.

Fit up the ticket office, and cloak room, with shelf and slide complete, as shown.

No. 27—STEPS.

Build wooden steps to the outside doors to King Street, as shown. The steps to be 1¼ inch, rises 1 inch, on strong carriages, with posts, rails, &c., all framed and fixed complete.

Build outside steps to four of the windows on each side of the Auditorium to descend to the side yard, all as shown; steps to be 1¼ inch, rises 1 inch, all supported on strong carriages and properly finished.

Fit up neatly with seats, risers, and hinged covers to all of the water closets. Fit up neatly about all basins, sinks, &c., and do all casing and carpenter's work connected with the plumbing, ventilating, &c., &c.

No. 28—TEMPORARY FLOOR.

There is to be a temporary floor provided to cover the Parquet to make a floor level with the floor of the stage. This floor is to be formed of 1¼ inch "white pine" flooring boards, put together in sections with strong battons nailed with wrought nails, the sections to be of convenient size to handle for putting in place and removing. These sections of floor will be supported on 3 inch by 6 inch scantlings set 2 feet between centers, the scantling to be supported on strong uprights or legs, of not more than 6 feet apart, all arranged and fixed in the most secure and convenient manner.

No. 29—SLATE ROOF.

Cover the steep part of the roof with the best quality Peach Bottom slates, laid on felting, and with a proper lap to secure tight roof, all as shown.

No. 30—TIN WORK.

Cover the roofs, dormars, cornices, &c., with the best quality I. C. charcoal brand bright roofing tin, perfectly welted and soldered in the best manner, turn the tin up and flash securely to the parapet walls and chimneys. Provide and put in large tin gutters, and tin conducting pipes of sufficient sizes to carry the water from the roof to the ground, all firmly secured.

No. 31—CRESTING.

Provide and set on the roof, iron crestings of the patterns shown by the drawings, all securely fixed.

No. 32—GAS PIPES.

Provide and lay gas pipes of suitable sizes, as per Gas Co.'s list, to light the various apartments throughout the entire building in the most approved manner. The main supply pipe to start in the basement or cellar, at convenient points to connect the meters; the pipes to be of the best quality, and laid in the best manner before plastering, and thoroughly tested; the outlets conveniently arranged for connecting the fixtures. There must be different meters for the different parts of the building.

No. 33—VENTILATING.

For summer ventilating there will be a large ventilator in the center of the ceiling over the Auditorium, as shown in the sections. There will be a venti-duct passing from this ventilator under the floor to the corridor, and through the space under the lantern between the Lodge rooms to the ventilating shaft.

For summer ventilation to the lodge rooms, and other rooms over the Auditorium and stage, there will be ventilators of proper size placed in the ceiling; two for each lodge room, and one for each of the other rooms, to communicate with the ventilating shaft above the ceiling.

The stage and the dressing rooms and other rooms under the stage will have summer ventilation by means of openings, and venti-ducts to the ventilating shaft, near the ceiling of the respective rooms. All of the ventilators must be provided with proper and convenient means of closing when requisite to do so. The ventilator over the Auditorium will be formed by means of perforations through the plaster ceiling, as shown.

Those in the other ceiling may be ornamental cast iron, set in the ceiling, and properly secured. Those for the large rooms should be at least 18 inches diameter, and the small rooms 12 inches diameter.

The venti-ducts will be formed of boards where boxing is required, and to be of proper sizes.

The stores, offices, &c., will have ventilation through the windows and doors, and lantern on the roof; the sash in the lantern to be hung on weights and cords, over pullies, and to be so arranged as to operate upon from below.

For winter ventilation it is proposed to take the air from the rear apartments at points on, or near the floor, by means of venti-ducts of proper sizes and suitably arranged to convey the air to the large ventilating or ejecting shaft, in which an upward current is to be maintained by the heat from the smoke pipe of the boiler, or if this is found insufficient on account of the distance of the boiler from the stack, then there must be a small stove, or gas jets, placed in the shaft to burn under iron hoods, to create sufficient heat to rarify the air, and cause an active upward current.

To ventilate the auditorium, stage, and rooms over the stage, there will be flues of 9 inches by 9 inches for the lower story, and 4 in. by 9 in. for the upper story; one to each of the brick piers, on each side of the building; these flues to connect with venti-ducts formed of boards and placed below the floors of each story, all as shown by the drawings. These venti-ducts all to be connected properly with the ejecting shaft.

There is to be an open ornamental enameled cast iron grating set to each of these flues just above the floors, to be firmly set flush with the plastering, all as will be directed.

No. 34—HEATING.

It is proposed to warm all parts of the rear building by a steam or hot water heating apparatus; that is, the Auditorium, and Stage and Lodge rooms, and other rooms in the upper story, and also the Banqueting room and Gymnasium in the upper story of the front building.

The boiler to be placed in the cellar under the Auditorium, and the warm air to be properly conveyed by pipes or tubes to the various apartments to be warmed, with all pipes, registers and fixtures complete. The apparatus to be of sufficient capacity to warm to a proper degree in the coldest weather, the various apartments that are to be warmed, and all arranged and fixed in the most approved, safe and convenient manner. The heating apparatus not to be included in the building contract, but the necessary flues to be built.

No. 35—PLUMBERS' WORK.

Provide and set patent valve water closets of the most approved kind, as follows, viz.: Eight in the basement story; four in the Principal story; six in the second, and four in the third story; set in the places indicated on the plans. These closets must be fitted up in the best maner, with all requisite fixtures complete; the traps to be of cast iron 5 inches diameter, and the soil from all the closets to be conveyed to the cesspool under the buildings, through cast iron soil-pipes of 5 inches diameter above ground, and terra-cotta under ground; and to be so arranged as not to be liable to choke or become obstructed, and each closet to have a proper supply of water.

Provide and set in the basement story, as shown, two large Bedfordshire urinals, with fixtures complete.

The cesspool to be ventilated through a 5 in. terra-cotta pipe laid under the cellar and basement floor from cesspool to the ventilating shaft, and to rise in the shaft to a point above the point where the smoke pipe comes in, and securely fixed.

No. 36—WASH BASINS.

Provide and set cast iron enameled wash hand basin, as follows, viz: Two in the basement; four in the principal story; and two in the second story: and cast iron enameled sinks as follows, viz.: Two in the basement, four in the principal story, and one in the second and one in the third story, all to have cast iron stands and fixtures complete, and set in the places indicated by the plans. The sinks to be supplied with water by a $\frac{5}{8}$ inch bibb cock, convenient for drawing water. There must be a $\frac{5}{8}$ inch bibb cock in the cellar, convenient for drawing water, and two patent street washers, one on Market Street and one on King Street, arranged at the most convenient points, and a suitable fire-plug set in a proper place in the orchestra. The waste from the urinals, sinks and basins must be carried to the soil-pipes, or to the side yard, through $1\frac{1}{4}$ inch medium lead pipes, all properly trapped, if connected with the soil pipes, and well fixed and secured. The closets, urinals, sinks, basins, bibb cocks, street washers and fire plug are all to be supplied with water from the city main.

The main supply pipes must be the best quality of galvanized iron $1\frac{1}{2}$ in. internal diam. and to each closet and bibb cock $\frac{3}{4}$ inch, and to each basin $\frac{1}{2}$ inch, with all requisite fixtures, fastenings &c., complete.

The floor under each water closet, sink, &c., wash hand basins must be lined with lead, three pounds to the foot superficial, to be turned up at least two inches on all sides, and large enough to catch all drips that may occur, and to have a $\frac{3}{4}$ inch pipe properly trapped into the soil pipe. There must be a separate stop cock to each water closet, sink and basin.

No. 37—PLASTERERS' WORK AND MATERIALS.

Lath the ceilings and stud partitions throughout, except that over the stage and in the attic or roof story, and the walls of the stage, and *including* the front basement and basement under the stage, with sound stiff laths; and put on two coats of brown mortar and a white coat or sand finish, as will be directed, to all of the walls. Lay on a heavy coat of mortar for counter ceiling over the auditorium and stage; partitions and ceilings, finish down to the floor in all cases. Square out and run straight or true to the curves shown, in the second coat, and float and trowel the white coat, or sand finish, to a hard finish, free from chip, or other cracks.

The columns, mouldings, &c., shown in the Proscenium Arch, and the mouldings around the center ventilator, to be formed in plaster, as shown.

Fresh wood burned lime, sharp grit sand, and sound hair to compose the mortar, to be mixed in proper proportions, and well tempered and prepared for use.

Provide and set to the flues in each store, office &c., a stove pipe collar.

No. 38—WALL COLORING AND DECORATIONS OR FRESCOING.

The walls and ceilings of the main entrance hall, the hall and stairways between the front and rear buildings, the Auditorium with all of its walls, ceilings, staircases, vestibules, &c., and all of the rooms, corridors, &c., of the top story, are to be colored in the distemper, the walls all to be plain, and the ceilings all to be properly decorated in the best style.

The contractor shall allow $1,200 for frescoing, and allow it to be done agreeable to the directions of the building committee.

No. 39—PAINTING AND GLAZING.

Glaze all of the sashes in the doors and windows throughout the building. The glass for the windows, doors and transoms of the stores to be French plate; and for the doors from the vestibule to the entrance hall, figured enameled glass, and for all the rest of the building first quality Waterford, N. J. or French cylinder glass, all well set, and tacked and glazed.

Paint all external and internal wood work usually painted, with three coats of oil paint. Grain all of the outside doors, and sash frames and sash on Market Street, in imitation of oak, or walnut, done in the best manner, and varnished with two coats. Paint all iron work usually painted, including the iron front, and the tin roof and spouting, with two coats of oil paint, the iron front to be finished white, or a very light color, and to have three coats of paint. Pure white lead and linseed oil to be used in the paints, properly prepared and laid on in such plain colors and in good full body as may be hereafter directed.

The stair-rails and balusters are all to be finished in oil. All iron work must have a coat of paint before being exposed to the weather.

The gallery front, the iron columns under the gallery front, and the fronts of the private boxes, will be finished with a pure white, to have an extra coat of paint, and to be decorated with slight touches of gilding, pricked in with blue and crimson, as will be directed. The cresting on the Mansard roof will be bronzed, and touched with gilding, as will be directed.

No. 40—FINALLY.

All the materials in the preceding specifications to be of the best of their several kinds, the lumber must be well seasoned, and all the workmanship to be executed in a neat, substantial, and workmanlike manner, to the true intent and meaning of the drawings and these specifications.

All the joists, girders and rafters to be cut prior to January 1st, 1871.

J. H. BEGGS,
J. P. ALLMOND, } Building Committee.
T. M. OGLE.

GEORCE G. LOBDELL, President Masonic Hall Co.

The Grand Experience was designed and seen through the press by Walnut Grove Graphic Design and Production Associates, Watkins Glen, New York. Its type was composed, paged, and reproduction proofs pulled by Tier Oldstyle Typesetting, Binghamton, N. Y. Color separations were done by Leo P. Callahan Color Service, Binghamton, N. Y. Camera work, stripping-in, presswork, and binding was performed by Valley Offset, Incorporated, Deposit, N. Y.

The types used were Goudy Titling, Goudy Oldstyle, Linotype Caslon, and Caslon Oldface.

The papers used were Finch Opaque Smooth and Strathmore Rhododendron Antique Cover.

An edition of two thousand copies was printed, of which three hundred were casebound in Skivertex Capra Ecrase and signed by the author.